Glitch

Glitch

The Hidden Impact of Faulty Software

Jeff Papows, Ph.D.

PRENTICE
HALL

Upper Saddle River, NJ • Boston • Indianapolis • San Francisco
New York • Toronto • Montreal • London • Munich • Paris • Madrid
Cape Town • Sydney • Tokyo • Singapore • Mexico City

Many of the designations used by manufacturers and sellers to distinguish their products are claimed as trademarks. Where those designations appear in this book, and the publisher was aware of a trademark claim, the designations have been printed with initial capital letters or in all capitals.

The author and publisher have taken care in the preparation of this book, but make no expressed or implied warranty of any kind and assume no responsibility for errors or omissions. No liability is assumed for incidental or consequential damages in connection with or arising out of the use of the information or programs contained herein.

The publisher offers excellent discounts on this book when ordered in quantity for bulk purchases or special sales, which may include electronic versions and/or custom covers and content particular to your business, training goals, marketing focus, and branding interests. For more information, please contact:

U.S. Corporate and Government Sales
800-382-3419
corpsales@pearsontechgroup.com

For sales outside the United States, please contact:

International Sales
international@pearson.com

Visit us on the Web: informit.com/ph

Library of Congress Cataloging-in-Publication Data:

Papows, Jeff.
  Glitch : the hidden impact of faulty software / Jeff Papows.
    p. cm.
  Includes bibliographical references.
  ISBN 978-0-13-216063-6
  1. Computer software--Quality control. 2. Manufactures--Defects. 3. Information technology--Management. I. Title.
  QA76.76.Q35P36 2010
  005--dc22
                              2010025053

ISBN-13: 978-0-132-16063-6
ISBN-10: 0-132-16063-3
Text printed in the United States on recycled paper at R.R. Donnelley in Crawfordsville, Indiana.
First printing September 2010

Associate Publisher
Greg Wiegand

Acquisitions Editor
Katherine Bull

Managing Editor
Kristy Hart

Project Editor
Jovana
San Nicolas-Shirley

Copy Editor
Gayle Johnson

Indexer
Lisa Stumpf

Proofreader
Water Crest
Publishing

**Publishing
Coordinator**
Cindy Teeters

Cover Designer
Alan Clements

Compositor
Nonie Ratcliff

Table of Contents

Foreword

Glitch might be too kind a word for too big a problem. In the technology industry, a glitch can be a simple, short, unnoticed interruption in a network connection or a file that gets saved in the wrong place. However, a glitch can also be as serious as life and death. The question isn't whether we need a new word to cover the span from short annoyances to major technology meltdowns, but how to avoid the glitch that can put you and your company in peril. That is the issue Jeff Papows, Ph.D., sets out to solve in this book.

The list of glitches Papows covers in this book is truly staggering. A driver in a serious car accident is able to dial 911, but a glitch prevents the nearest fire department from being alerted to the emergency. A motorist stops to buy a pack of cigarettes and finds a charge for $23 quadrillion and change on his bank statement. What started as a simple software upgrade at a nuclear power plant spirals into an automatic, unplanned shutdown.

These and many other glitch stories are part of this book, but a simple list of glitches would not help solve this very big problem. Where Papows distinguishes himself is in writing a book that does not simply accept computer and technology problems as an unalterable happenstance, but as the end result of a faulty set of business and technology practices. It was the idea that computer shutdowns and other assorted malfunctions are not just part of doing business that attracted me to Papows' manuscript and why I was happy to be asked to write this Foreword.

In my course of covering the technology industry as a journalist for over twenty years, I've had the opportunity to write a lot about computer glitches, bugs, and major meltdowns, from the ILOVEYYOU worm in 2000 that coursed through Windows systems via email to the cascade of business process and technology failures that prevented BP from detecting and preventing the disastrous oil rig blowout currently devastating the Gulf of Mexico. Too often, in my opinion, these and other technology meltdowns are seen as an act of inevitable happenstance at best or a dire, but acceptable, consequence of technology advance, which is a regrettable but necessary part of scientific progress. Papows shows both those scenarios to be wrongheaded and a result of faulty thinking rather than faulty electronic widgets or software programs.

What this book accomplishes is to provide a guide to business and technology managers wanting not only to root out and prevent glitches before they strangle a company's financial life, but also allowing technology advances to improve our society. Creating a society without the fear of a technology-based disaster unfolding just one glitch away would be a remarkable and noble achievement.

Although, as Papows explains in detail, there is not a simple "anti-glitch" piece of electronic wizardry to prevent future technology malfunctions, there are a set of predefined skills and business processes a company can wield to protect itself against headline-grabbing technology meltdowns. One of the greatest contributions of this book is to call on technology educators and industry to think big and redefine the roles of the software engineer, restructure information technology governance, and create business processes where technology is used to accelerate an idea into a product or service offered to the public without a company killing lurking glitches unseen. One of the strongest pieces of advice that Papows offers is to embrace mistakes early and often in the technology development process as a way to squash those minor bugs before they grow to the size of business-killing problems. The steps he offers in killing those minor bugs before they become major issues don't require advanced technology degrees or enormous capital investments, but do require that all parties speak a common business language, have a common set of goals, and discard finger-pointing blame sessions in favor of producing a bug-free product or service. It is in explaining how to create that bug-free environment that Papows offers a unique and important contribution to business and government leaders.

The timing of this book could not be more important. As a society, we sit aghast as we watch a digital video feed of spilled oil fouling major fisheries and pristine beaches. Meanwhile, as our personal and business lives become ever more intertwined in online social networks, and vital business operations now take place in a computing cloud, business and individual life depend on technology operations to run flawlessly 24 hours a day. Preventing glitches from disrupting or destroying our digital-dependent society is what this book is all about, and it's worth your time to read and understand Papows prescription to keep those nasty computer bugs at bay.

Eric Lundquist
Vice President, Strategic Content
Ziff Davis Enterprise

Acknowledgments

When CEOs extend their focus to writing a book, they must rely on smart, dedicated staff to help them balance the demands of writing with the responsibilities of running their business. These people inevitably become key contributors to the quality of the final work, whether through research assistance, editing expertise, or giving the author an occasional sanity check.

After writing *Enterprise.com*, I knew that the work needed for *Glitch* would require support and collaboration from key individuals. Two of these individuals have worked with me for decades, beginning at Lotus and continuing at Maptuit and now WebLayers.

My deepest thanks go to Sharon Ricci and Carlos Bernal for their professional dedication and friendship over the decades, as well as for inspiring me to write this book. Getting from inspiration to the chapters published here required much assistance in fact-checking a wide array of information, identifying and interviewing topical experts, and organizing and editing the final content. Kathleen Keating collaborated on these and numerous other activities with great urgency so as to meet our ambitious deadline. I thank them, along with John Favazza, WebLayers' VP of research and development, for their assiduousness in keeping *Glitch* on track.

I also wish to thank several other people who made this book possible. My acquisitions editor at Pearson Education, Katherine Bull, believed in *Glitch* and made others believe as well, and Jovana San Nicolas-Shirley helped make the production of *Glitch* a painless undertaking. Importantly, I also want to thank Joe McKendrick and Esther Schindler—two very insightful people whose knowledge and feedback during the manuscript review made *Glitch* a better book.

Words cannot express the gratitude I have for the support and contributions of all these key professionals.

I tend to talk at length about the people-centric nature of the software industry and why I have enjoyed that aspect of this business the most. Many thanks are due to the tremendous people who have shared their finest accomplishments and their valuable friendships with me over the years as employees, institutional investors, and industry colleagues.

I will close by expressing my appreciation to you, the reader, as well as to the many brilliant, diligent, caring, and resourceful people who will tackle the IT governance challenges presented in this book.

About the Author

Jeff Papows, Ph.D., President and CEO of WebLayers, has more than 30 years of industry experience and a proven history of success in both emerging companies and large global organizations. Most notably, he was President and CEO of Lotus Development Corporation. There he was widely credited with taking Lotus Notes from its initial release to sales of more than 80 million copies worldwide, making it the leading collaboration platform. After Lotus was acquired, Papows helped steer the company's successful integration into IBM. He also was President of Cognos Corporation, taking the business intelligence software provider from its early stages to sustained profitability, a public offering, and continued growth that met or exceeded Wall Street expectations.

Most recently, Papows was President and CEO of Maptuit, a provider of real-time commercial navigation software. Having led Maptuit to profitability and a market leadership position, he continues to play an active role in the company as Chairman of the Board.

Papows has been a frequent guest on CNN and Fox News and is a successful author. His book *Enterprise.com: Information Leadership in the Digital Age* has been reprinted in several languages. He holds a Ph.D. in business administration as well as a master of arts degree and a bachelor of science degree.

CHAPTER 1

Converging Forces

On July 15, 2009, 22-year-old New Hampshire resident Josh Muszynski swiped his debit card at a local gas station to purchase a pack of cigarettes. A few hours later, while checking his bank balance online, Muszynski discovered that he had been charged $23,148,855,308,184,500.00 for the cigarettes, as shown in Figure 1.1.[1]

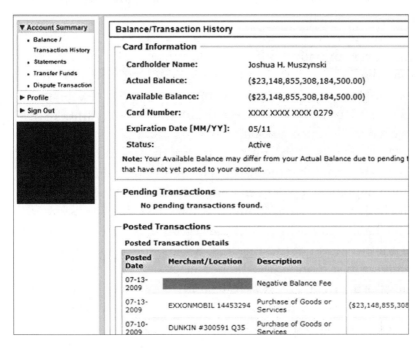

Figure 1.1   *Josh Muszynski's bank statement*

That's twenty-three quadrillion, one hundred forty-eight trillion, eight hundred fifty-five billion, three hundred eight million, one hundred eighty-four thousand, five hundred dollars. Plus the $15 overdraft fee charged by the bank. This is about 2,007 times the U.S. national debt.

In a statement from Visa, the issuer of Muszynski's debit card, what had happened to Muszynski, along with "fewer than 13,000 prepaid transactions," resulted from a "temporary programming error at Visa Debit Processing Services … which caused some transactions to be inaccurately posted to a small number of Visa prepaid accounts." In a follow-up statement, customers were assured "that the problem has been fixed and that all falsely issued fees have been voided. Erroneous postings have been removed … this incident had no financial impact on Visa prepaid cardholders."

No financial impact. It's hard to believe that this incident had no impact on Muszynski, considering that he had to go back and forth between the debit card issuer and the bank to address the situation.

Although the issue was settled after a few days, Muszynski was never formally notified of the cause of the error aside from the information he discovered by doing an Internet search. He saw that the $23 quadrillion cigarette charge and overdraft fee had been corrected only after he continuously checked the balance himself.

When I spoke with Muszynski about the situation,[2] he said, "I was surprised that they even let it go through at first. Then, after it happened, I was even more surprised that I was the one who had to notify them about it." Muszynski is still a customer of the bank, but now he checks his account balance every day. As another result of this incident, he has shifted his spending behavior to a more old-fashioned approach: "I now pay for things using cash. I used to rely on my debit card, but it's just easier and safer for me to go to the bank and take cash out for what I need."

Now that's something every bank that's making a killing in ATM transaction fees wants to hear—a customer would rather stand in line for face-to-face service than risk being on the receiving end of another glitch.

Glitches Are More Than Inconveniences

Barely a day goes by where we don't hear about one or more computer errors that affect tens of thousands of people all over the world. In the content of this book, when we address glitches, it is from the perspective of software development and its impact on businesses and consumers. More specifically, it's about the way that software is developed and managed and how inconcistent approaches and methodologies can lead to gaps in the software code that compromises the quality of product or services that is ultimately delivered to the customer.

Unless these types of glitches affect us directly, we tend to shrug and write them off. For consumers who are grounded in an airport for several hours or who are reported as being late on their mortgage payments, these types of computer errors have a much longer and far more public impact thanks to the rise of social media tools such as Twitter and Facebook. A quick Google search revealed that the story of the $23 quadrillion pack of cigarettes appeared in more than 44,800 media outlets, including newspapers, blogs, radio, and television.

For the businesses servicing these customers, the cost of addressing these types of issues goes beyond brand damage control. This is because what can initially appear to be an anomaly can actually be a widespread error that is staggeringly expensive to fix. These unanticipated costs can include extensive software redevelopment or the need to bring down systems for hours, if not days, to uncover the underlying causes and to halt further mistakes.

Although charts and tables can try to estimate the cost of downtime to an organization, it's difficult to quantify the impact because of many variables such as size of company, annual revenues, and compliance violation fines.

According to a research note written by IT industry analyst Bill Malik of Gartner, a Stamford, Connecticut-based technology analyst firm, "Any outage assessment based on raw, generic industry averages alone is misleading." The most effective way to gauge the cost of downtime, according to Gartner, is to estimate the cost of an outage to your firm by calculating lost revenue, lost profit, and staff cost for an average hour—and for a worst-case hour—of downtime for each critical business process.[3]

What's Behind the Glitches?

Given how much technology has evolved, we have to ask why these software glitches continue to happen. Why are we seeing more glitches instead of fewer? And now that technology is pervasive in our business and personal lives, how do we make sure that we're not the cause or the victim of one of these hidden threats that may take days, weeks, or months to unravel?

Flight delays, banking errors, and inaccurate record keeping are just some of the millions of glitches that affect consumers and businesses all over the world. However, when you consider the amount of technology that's in place at companies of every size all over the world, it's easy to see how these glitches make their way into our computer systems. We've already seen the effects of these types of glitches. What will be different in the future is that they will be more widespread and affect more people due to our increased connectedness and reliance on technology. The result will be more costly and time-consuming outages because the glitches will be harder to detect among the millions of lines of software code that allow us to connect to the office and with our friends all over the globe.

How did we get to this point, and why am I convinced that these issues and many like them will, in fact, happen? The simple answer is that many IT professionals have unwittingly created an industry so hyper-focused on the next big thing that we have taken some shortcuts in the creation of solid foundations—otherwise known in the IT world as infrastructures—that will firmly support us in the future. In these situations, the actions that lead to these glitches are not deliberate. What typically happens is that shortcuts are taken during the software development process to accelerate product release cycles with the goal of boosting revenues. While that's the simple explanation, the issue obviously is more complex.

Three of the most pressing drivers are

- Loss of intellectual knowledge
- Market consolidation
- The ubiquity of technology

Although at first these may appear to be disparate forces, they actually are intertwined.

Loss of Intellectual Knowledge

First, let's cover the basics of the intellectual knowledge issue. As computers became part of the business landscape, the mainframe was the de facto standard for financial institutions, government agencies, and insurance companies. These entities continue to rely on these fast and stable workhorses to keep their operations running. Software developers programmed mainframes using a language called COBOL (common business-oriented language).

Half a century later, COBOL is still going strong, because mainframes are still the backbone of 75 percent of businesses and government agencies according to industry analysts at Datamonitor.[4] Of that 75 percent, 90 percent of global financial transactions are processed in COBOL. Yet as different and more modern languages were introduced to reflect the evolution of technology, there was less emphasis and, frankly, less incentive for the next generation to learn COBOL.

As the lines of COBOL code continued to grow over the years, the number of skilled programmers has steadily declined. It's difficult to quantify the number of active COBOL programmers currently employed. In 2004, the last time Gartner tried to count COBOL programmers, the consultancy estimated that there were approximately two million worldwide and the number was declining at 5 percent annually.[5]

The greatest impact of COBOL programmers leaving the workforce will be felt from 2015 through 2029. This makes sense when you realize that the oldest of the baby boomer generation are those born between 1946 and 1950 and that this generation will approach the traditional retirement age of 65 between the years 2011 and 2015.[6]

As these workers prepare for retirement or are part of a generation that doesn't stay at one company for their entire career, last-minute scrambles to capture a career's worth of programming expertise and how it's been applied to company-specific applications are challenging.

However, efforts are under way to address this issue. They include IBM's Academic Initiative and the Academic Connection (ACTION) program from Micro Focus International plc, a software company that helps modernize COBOL applications. Both programs are actively involved in teaching COBOL skills at colleges and universities worldwide. However, very little was done to document the knowledge of these skilled workers in the real world while they were on the job.

The COBOL Skills Debate

It's debatable whether a COBOL skills shortage actually exists. To some degree, the impact of the dearth of skilled workers will depend on how many of a company's applications rely on COBOL.

For companies that will be affected, industry analysts at Gartner published a report in 2010 titled "Ensuring You Have Mainframe Skills Through 2020."[7] In the report, Gartner analysts advise companies that depend on mainframes how to prepare for the impending skills shortage. The report says companies should work closely with human resources professionals to put a comprehensive plan in place that will help guide them through the next decade, when the mainframe skills shortage will be more prominent.

Mike Chuba, a vice president at Gartner and author of the report, wrote, "Many organizations have specialists with years of deep knowledge—a formal plan to capture and pass on that knowledge via cross-training or mentoring of existing personnel is critical."

From a day-to-day perspective, the inability to sufficiently support the mainframe could have a significant impact on the economy. Micro Focus International plc has found that COBOL applications are involved in transporting up to 72,000 shipping containers, caring for 60 million patients, processing 80 percent of point-of-sale transactions, and connecting 500 million mobile phone users.[8]

According to Kim Kazmaier, a senior IT architect with over 30 years of industry experience, this skills challenge is the result of a combination of factors: "The demographics have changed. You are unlikely to find many people who remain in one company, industry, or technology focus for long periods of time, unlike previous generations of IT professionals. Also, the sheer volume and complexity of technology make it virtually impossible for any individual to master the information about all the technology that's in use within a large IT organization. It used to be that an IT professional would literally study manuals cover to cover, but those days have been replaced by just-in-time learning."

"To be fair, the information that once filled a bookcase would now fill entire rooms. We simply don't have the luxury to master that much information individually, so we rely on information mash-ups provided by collaboration, search engines, metadata repositories, and often overstretched subject-matter experts."

How to Prepare for Any Pending Skills Drought

This issue adds up to fewer skilled IT workers to handle the increasing issues of developing and managing software, which results in the proliferation of glitches.

How can organizations address this issue in a logical and realistic way? The most practical approach—and one that can be applied to nearly any challenge of this nature—is to first fully understand the business issue, and then figure out how your people can help address it through technology.

The first step is to conduct an IT audit by invoking a comprehensive inventory of all the technology in the infrastructure. Along with tracking all the COBOL-specific applications, you should understand which non-COBOL applications intersect with COBOL applications. Given that we are more connected every day, applications are no longer relegated to specific departments or companies. Because COBOL is behind a significant number of business transactions, there is a strong likelihood that the non-COBOL applications being created today will also pass through a mainframe. The inventory process is actually not as arduous as it may initially seem, given the amount of available technology resources that can accelerate this step.

The next step is to get an update on the percentage of COBOL expertise in your company versus other technologies, as well as tenure and retirement dates. Based on an IT audit and staff evaluation, you can get a clear picture of just how much of a risk the COBOL situation is to your organization.

If you determine that your company is at risk due to a lack of COBOL expertise, consider the following recommendations:

- Be realistic about knowledge transfer
- Cross-train staff
- Automate as much as possible

Be Realistic About Knowledge Transfer

A logical course of action would be to suggest knowledge transfer, but that won't completely resolve the situation because of two significant issues. The first is that the applications that were put in place decades ago have been consistently tweaked, updated, and enhanced through the years. It would be impossible to review every change made along the way to pick up exactly where a COBOL expert with 30 years of experience left off. This won't be a showstopper, but it can result in longer-than-expected cycles to identify the source of a glitch.

This leads to the second issue—experience. It's simply not possible to do a Vulcan mind meld with the retiring workforce and expect a new team of developers to be as conversant in COBOL as people who have dedicated their careers to it. Although knowledge transfer is important, companies should be realistic in their expectations.

Cross-Train Staff

There's no reason that the IT job of the future couldn't or shouldn't be a hybrid of various kinds of technology expertise. For example, you could offer positions that mix different skill sets such as Flash programming and COBOL and offer additional salary and benefits to the cross-trained developers. This would result in greater expertise across the company and would help you avoid creating knowledge silos.

Automate Where Possible

If your company is facing a skills shortage, consider using technology to automate as many tasks as possible. You can never fully replace intellectual knowledge, but this step can help alleviate the time-consuming and less-strategic functions that still need to happen on a regular basis.

Computer Science Is Cool Again

Whether or not you believe that a pending COBOL skills drought is imminent, you can't deny that there is a demand for IT skills across the board. The U.S. Bureau of Labor Statistics (BLS) estimates that by 2018, the information sector will create more than one million jobs. The BLS includes the following areas in this category: data processing, web and application hosting, streaming services, Internet publishing, broadcasting, and software publishing.[9] Although this represents great opportunities for the next generation, we will face a supply-and-demand issue when it comes to building and maintaining the technology that runs our businesses.

This is due to the fact that the number of students studying computer science and related disciplines at the college and university level is just now on the upswing after steadily declining from 2000 to 2007, largely as a result of the dotcom collapse. In March 2009, *The New York Times*[10] reported on the Computing Research Association Taulbee Survey. It found that as of 2008, enrollment in computer science programs increased for the first time in six years, by 6.2 percent.[11] But the gap will still exist from nearly a decade of students who opted out of studying the fundamentals associated with software design, development, and programming. Adding to this is the evidence that students studying computer science today are more interested in working with "cooler" front-end application technologies—the more visible and lucrative aspects in the industry. They're not as interested in the seemingly less-exciting opportunities associated with the mainframe. The Taulbee Survey found that part of the resurgence in studying computer science is due to the excitement surrounding social media and mobile technologies.

Market Consolidation

The next factor that is creating this perfect storm is mergers and consolidation. Although market consolidation is part of the natural ebb and flow of any industry, a shift has occurred in the business model of mergers and consolidation. It is driven by larger deals and the need to integrate more technology.

From an IT perspective, when any two companies merge, the integration process is often much lengthier and more time-consuming than originally anticipated. This holds true regardless of the merger's size. Aside from the integration of teams and best practices, there is the very real and potentially very costly process of making the two different IT infrastructures work together.

One of the biggest "hurry up" components of mergers is the immediacy of combining the back-office systems of the new collective entity. At a minimum, similar if not duplicate applications will be strewn throughout the infrastructure of both companies. With all these variations on the same type of application, such as customer accounts, sales databases, and human resources files, there will undoubtedly be inconsistencies in how the files were created. These inconsistencies become very apparent during the integration process. For example, John Q. Customer may be listed as both J.Q. Customer and Mr. John Customer and might have duplicate entries associated with different addresses and/or accounts, yet all of those accounts represent one customer.

Along with trying to streamline the number of applications is the challenge of integrating the various technologies that may or may not adhere to industry standards. Getting all the parts of the orchestra to play the right notes at the right time presents a significant challenge for even the most talented IT professionals.

From a more mainstream point of view, spotty efforts to merge infrastructures can have a very real impact on consumers. For example, according to the Boston, Massachusetts television station and NBC affiliate WHDH, as well as the local Boston CW news affiliate, when tuxedo retailers Mr. Tux and Men's Wearhouse merged in 2007, a computer glitch didn't properly track inventory and customer orders.[12] This resulted in wedding parties and others on their way to formal events without their preordered tuxedos. Since you can't change the date of such events, many customers had to incur additional expenses by going to another vendor to ensure they were properly attired for their big day.

Before you start chuckling at the thought of groomsmen wearing tuxedo T-shirts instead of formal wear, keep in mind that the U.S. wedding industry represents $86 billion annually[13] and that men's formal wear represents $250 million annually.[14] Talk about a captive audience—you can well imagine the word-of-mouth influence of an entire wedding reception.

Hallmarks of Successful Mergers

Every company that's been through a merger can share its own tales of what went right, what went wrong, and what never to do again. Yet I believe that successful mergers have consistent hallmarks:

- A *cross-functional team:* This group is dedicated to the success of the merger. It needs to represent all the different functions of the newly formed organization and should work on the integration full time.

- A *realistic road map:* When millions of dollars are at stake, especially if one or both of the companies are publicly traded, there may be a tendency to set aggressive deadlines to accelerate the integration. Don't sacrifice the quality of the efforts and the customer experience for short-term financial gains. For example, if your senior-level IT staff tells you the deadlines are unrealistic, listen carefully and follow their lead.

- *Humility:* Don't assume that the acquiring organization has the better infrastructure and staff. Part of the responsibility of the integration team is to take a closer look at all the resources that are now available to create the strongest company possible.

- *Technology overlap:* Whether a successful integration takes three months or three years, do not shut off any systems until the merger is complete from an IT perspective. You may need to spend more resources to temporarily keep simultaneous systems running, but this is well worth the investment to avoid any disruptions in service to customers.

- *Anticipate an extensive integration process.* The biggest mistake an acquiring company can make is to assume that the integration will be complete in 90 days. Although it may be complete from a legal and technical standpoint, don't overlook the commitment required from a cultural perspective or you may risk degrading the intellectual value of the acquisition.

The Ubiquity of Technology

The third force that is contributing to the impending IT storm is the sheer volume and ubiquity of technology that exists among both businesses and consumers. It's difficult to understate the scale at which the IT industry has transformed productivity, stimulated economic growth, and forever changed how people work and live.

It's hard to overlook the contributions of the information technology sector to the gross domestic product (GDP). Even with the natural expansion and contractions in the economy, the IT sector continues to be a growth engine. In 2007, U.S. businesses spent $264.2 billion on information and communication technology (ICT) equipment and computer software, representing a 4.4 percent increase over the year 2006.[15]

The next decade shows no signs of stopping. A February 2010 Internet and mobile growth forecast jointly developed by IT networking vendor Cisco and independent analysts said that global Internet traffic growth is expected to reach 56 exabytes (EB) per month. The various forms of video, including TV, video on demand (VOD), Internet video, and peer-to-peer (P2P), will exceed 90 percent of global consumer traffic. This will all happen by the year 2013. The same report forecast that the mobile industry will realize a compounded annual growth rate of 108 percent per year through the year 2014. Figure 1.2 shows Cisco's forecast for mobile data growth in terabytes (TB) and exabytes.[16]

I often equate technology with fire: It can warm your hands on a cold night, or it can burn down your house. The innovations of the past few decades illustrate this point. They've resulted in a massive amount of software and devices that, if not properly developed and managed, can bring down a network and shut out those who rely on it.

The irony is that the technology industry has created and perpetuated the ubiquity of its products, which is leading to this potential perfect storm of sorts.

Does this mean that a technology Armageddon is under way? Well, that's a bit dramatic, but it's not too far from what could potentially happen if we continue to allow these technology glitches to fester in our infrastructures.

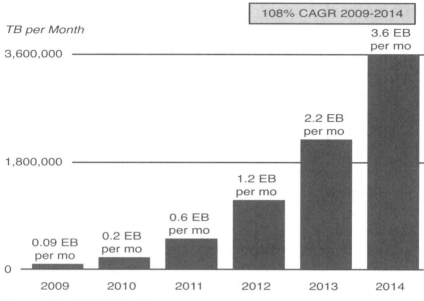

Source: Cisco VNI Mobile, 2010

Figure 1.2   *Cisco VNI mobile growth*

Endnotes

1. Bank of America Statement. Josh Muszynski.

2. Interview with Josh Muszynski by Kathleen Keating and Barbara McGovern. December 2009.

3. Gartner. "Q&A: How Much Does an Hour of Downtime Cost?" Bill Malik. September 29, 2009.

4. Datamonitor. "COBOL: Continuing to Drive Value in the 21st Century." Alan Roger, et al. November 2008.

5. *Computerworld*. "Confessions of a COBOL Programmer." Tam Harbert. February 20, 2008. http://www.computerworld.com/s/article/print/9062478/Confessions_of_a_Cobol_programmer?taxonomyName=Web+Services&taxonomyId=61.

6. Forrester Research. "Academic Programs Are Beginning to Offset Anticipated Mainframe Talent Shortages." Phil Murphy with Alex Cullen and Tim DeGennaro. March 19, 2008.

7. Gartner. "Ensuring You Have Mainframe Skills Through 2020." Mike Chuba. April 5, 2010.

8. Micro Focus International plc. http://www.itworldcanada.com/news/action-program-makes-cobol-cool-again/140364.

9. Bureau of Labor Statistics. Occupational Outlook Handbook, 2010–2011 Edition. Overview of the 2008–2018 Projections. December 17, 2009. http://www.bls.gov/oco/oco2003.htm#industry.

10. *The New York Times.* "Computer Science Programs Make a Comeback in Enrollment." John Markoff. March 16, 2009. http://www.nytimes.com/2009/03/17/science/17comp.html.

11. Computer Research Association. Taulbee Survey. http://www.cra.org/resources/taulbee/.

12. 7News WHDH. "Company Merger and Computer Glitch Delays Tuxedos." October 13, 2007. http://www1.whdh.com/news/articles/local/BO64447/.

13. Association for Wedding Professionals International, Sacramento, CA. Richard Markel.

14. International Formalwear Association, Galesburg, IL. Ken Pendley, President.

15. U.S. Census Bureau. Press release. Business Spending on Information and Communication Technology Infrastructure Reaches $264 Billion in 2007. February 26, 2009. http://www.census.gov/Press-Release/www/releases/archives/economic_surveys/013382.html.

16. Cisco Visual Networking Index: Global Mobile Data Traffic Forecast Update 2009–2014. http://www.cisco.com/en/US/solutions/collateral/ns341/ns525/ns537/ns705/ns827/white_paper_c11-520862.html.

CHAPTER 2

The Personal Impact

Glitches have become quite commonplace in headlines and in our personal lives. We usually don't pay attention to them or are no longer surprised when they happen—unless it is something so massive and dangerous that it disrupts our lives.

Because we are pouring more technology into automobiles and medical devices, it is not a stretch to say that glitches can sometimes be a matter of life and death. This chapter explores the issues surrounding Toyota vehicle recalls, as well as the impact of faulty technology on radiation machines designed to help treat cancer patients.

From there, we'll address the role that consumers, business leaders, and government officials can and should take to help reduce the impact of these life-threatening computing errors.

Toyota: From Class Act to Class Action

Toyota, the world's largest auto manufacturer,[1] is one company whose glitches have been front and center. Once it was a symbol of quality and safety. But Toyota's reputation took a nosedive when the company was forced to recall vehicles as news of deaths and injuries to drivers made headlines around the world. This bad publicity was most prevalent throughout the latter half of 2009 and the first half of 2010.

On January 21, Toyota announced the first in a series of product recalls that would occur throughout 2010, and prompt government action. The first voluntary recall of the year was for 2.3 million vehicles across eight of its brands that were manufactured between 2005 and 2010. The recall was due to accelerator pedals that may mechanically stick in a partially depressed position or return slowly to the idle position.[2] Essentially, Toyota issued the recall to warn owners that the vehicles may accelerate or decelerate on their own. Five days later, Toyota suspended the sales of the potentially affected models.[3]

On January 27, dealing with a separate issue related to accelerator defects, Toyota sent a letter to the United States National Highway Traffic Safety Administration (NHTSA). In the letter, Toyota amended its Defect Information Report that was filed on October 5, 2009, stating the potential risk for floor mat entrapment of accelerator pedals in certain Toyota and Lexus models.[4] What could potentially happen in the instances outlined in the recall is that the accelerator pedal gets trapped in the floor mat and continues to increase the vehicle's speed while diminishing the driver's ability to control the automobile. As a side note, it is the auto manufacturer's legal responsibility to alert the NHTSA within five days of discovering a product defect.

Pedal entrapment is exactly what happened to the Saylor family of Chula Vista, California. Mark Saylor, his wife Cloefe, their 13-year-old daughter, Mahala, and Cloefe's brother, Chris Lastrella, were on their way to Mahala's soccer practice in a Lexus ES350 on August 28, 2009. When the car's accelerator got caught in the floor mat, Mark Saylor couldn't control the vehicle as it quickly accelerated to over 100 miles per hour. The car went through an intersection on a dead-end road, sideswiped another car, crashed through a fence, landed in a riverbed, and burst into flames. Unfortunately, there were no survivors.[5] The tragedy of the Saylor family was one of many incidents involving Toyota vehicles; the majority of reports cited problems with the car's accelerator.

The issues for Toyota escalated after the United States Department of Transportation received several complaints about braking difficulties in the 2010 Toyota Prius hybrids.

This led to the February 4, 2010 opening of an investigation into Toyota by the Department of Transportation.[6] Four days later, Toyota announced a voluntary safety recall on approximately 133,000 2010 model year Prius vehicles and 14,400 Lexus Division 2010 HS 250h vehicles so that Toyota could update the software in the antilock brake system (ABS).

According to the formal statement issued by Toyota, "Some 2010 model year Prius and 2010 HS 250h owners have reported experiencing inconsistent brake feel during slow and steady application of brakes on rough or slick road surfaces when the ABS (antilock brake system) is activated in an effort to maintain tire traction."[7]

The bottom line with the Prius recall is an issue with the software.[8] The Toyota recalls continued across the company's various brands due to additional mechanical issues that were categorized as glitches until a fuller investigation could be conducted.

The U.S. Government Gets in the Driver's Seat

Toyota's successive product recalls—more than eight million vehicles in 2010—led to fuller investigations by the U.S. government, including the U.S. Department of Transportation[9] and the U.S. House Committee on Oversight and Government Reform.[10]

The prepared testimony delivered by Toyota President and CEO Akio Toyoda echoes the issues that are facing many companies today, not just auto manufacturers. In his statement before the U.S. House Committee on Oversight and Government Reform, he said, "Toyota has, for the past few years, been expanding its business rapidly. Quite frankly, I fear the pace at which we have grown may have been too quick." He added, "We pursued growth over the speed at which we were able to develop our people and our organization, and we should sincerely be mindful of that."[11]

Like many companies that are in the midst of continued growth, it's easy to lose sight of the fundamentals that are baked into the technology and are the catalyst for that growth. Anecdotally, if you've ever been through a downsizing, you've likely heard the mantras about getting back to basics and focusing on what matters. If we could sustain that mind-set regardless of fluctuations in the economy, we might see less technology-related catastrophes that result from failing to focus on the right things.

The massive Toyota recalls prompted the U.S. House Energy and Commerce Committee to propose to Congress the Motor Vehicle Safety Act of 2010.[12] From a technology point of view, the bill suggests several improvements to how vehicles are designed, engineered, tested, and manufactured. It also makes provisions for the inclusion of "event data recorders" that will be included in every automobile starting in 2012. These event data recorders are a scaled-down version of airplane black boxes. They are designed to help provide more accurate reporting in the event of a crash or air bag deployment.

Financial Implications

Toyota is facing hefty government fines, along with recall costs and lawsuits. Not the least of these line items was the $16.375 million fine imposed by NHTSA, the maximum fine allowed, for failure to notify it of the pedal defect for almost four months.[13]

Toyota's final tally from these glitches has yet to be determined, although estimates range from $3 to $5 billion. The actual costs will vary, depending on class-action lawsuits that include death and serious-injury claims. Also, deeper investigations will occur into previous accidents that may have erroneously been categorized as driver error as opposed to gas pedal malfunction. These are just the tip of the iceberg for Toyota when you think about the impact of automobile resale value, car dealers' bottom lines, insurers that paid claims where Toyota was ultimately responsible, and so on.

However, let's not be fooled into thinking that the issues at Toyota are isolated and are not part of the larger, industry-wide technology issues that are looming. The overwhelming public concern is quite valid, and Toyota has issued subsequent apologies and updates to show how it's addressing the problems. However, I suspect that Toyota won't be the only auto manufacturer to face such a public flogging because of software glitches.

Lessons Learned from Toyota

As more automobiles are instrumented with technology, it's important to keep the lessons learned from Toyota top of mind. Three critical lessons can be learned from this situation:

- Be forthcoming about potential product issues, even if they haven't yet resulted in injury. Contributing to Toyota's image problem as well as the financial toll was Toyota's delayed response to the accelerator issue.

- Success and continued company growth need to be carefully managed and aligned with technology processes that are focused on the customer. This is especially true with manufacturing products that can affect a consumer's quality of life.

- We need a more effective way of testing and introducing new technology into automobiles. Just as you need a license to drive, I propose that we apply that same principle to the engineers who design and develop technology. We could require a stringent technology licensing, certification, and renewal process for IT governance in the automobile industry.

The Technology Behind the Wheel

The technology that's included in automobiles these days, such as global positioning systems, keyless entry, and parking assistance, is brilliant. As much as we like to think that embedding technology in automobiles is a relatively new idea, it's been happening for decades, for better and for worse.

Based on data from the NHTSA, since the introduction of technology into vehicles 30 years ago, the number of electronic system recalls in the U.S. has tripled.[14] This isn't surprising considering that IT analysts at Frost & Sullivan report that a modern luxury car contains close to 100 million lines of software code. Who'd have thought that much technology would be required to pick up a gallon of milk and a loaf of bread?

Considering that we've become accustomed to having our appliances, computers, and devices fully loaded, it only makes sense that we apply those same wants and needs to our vehicles.

The advances in automotive engineering and design as well as IT will only continue to increase the amount of technology we embed in vehicles. A look into the future reveals that we've only just begun to explore the inclusion of massive amounts of technology in our automobiles.

We may have adjusted to the idea of allowing a DVD player in our vehicles to occupy the kids on long rides, but are we ready to allow the Internet into our cars? We'd better be if the analysts at market research firm iSuppli are correct in their prediction that by 2016, 62.3 million global consumers will have Internet access in their cars.[15] Figure 2.1 illustrates the expected growth of Internet-connected cars.

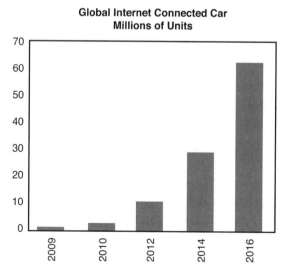

Figure 2.1   *Global Internet-connected cars 2009–2016.*

The safety implications of having an Internet browser on our automobile dashboards present their own set of issues. This rings especially true when you consider that in 2008 nearly 6,000 people died and more than half a million people were injured in crashes involving a distracted driver.[16]

I suspect automobile manufacturers will put legally approved warnings in place to protect them from the fallout that's likely to come when you allow car owners to simultaneously drive and surf. Yet these types of innovations call into question whether we are using technology to add value on behalf of the consumer or simply doing it because we can.

Although distracted drivers are not directly linked to glitches, what you have to remember is that the addition of more technology into an automobile—even to ease the driving experience—can increase the propensity of glitches.

Due Diligence for Enterprise Software Procurement

As a culture, we're inundated with marketing messages designed to convince us that the latest and greatest widget will change our lives, solve our business problems, make us smarter, and transform us overnight. The IT industry is no exception. Because much of the enterprise-class software that we're talking about is complex, distinguishing the buzzwords from the actual business value that the product delivers is not always easy.

Even after thorough product testing, evaluations, and what's known as proof of concept (POC), which puts the product through its paces in the customer's real-world environment, mixed or failed results can occur after significant financial and intellectual investments have been made.

To help filter quality products from the latest marketing campaigns, the following seven criteria should be part of the due diligence process:

- *Think like a customer.* You often hear people in the IT industry talk about aligning technology with business goals. Although this is important, the customer should be the priority. In a globally connected world, competition can come from anywhere, and loyalty is rooted in the quality of service that the customer receives. If the conversation you're having with the IT vendor goes down the road of how the software can do wild and crazy things like streamline business processes, ask the vendor how this benefits your customer. For every feature and benefit that is pitched, respond with questions about the value to the customer.

■ *Don't just buy; invest.* Consider the decision to buy technology an investment, not a static purchase, because the technology will continue to evolve and improve just as your company does. For enterprise software, you can expect the value of the investment to become clear within 18 to 24 months. For technology that is more consumer-oriented in nature, such as subscription-based tax preparation software, the same principles apply, although the return on investment is more immediate. In both scenarios, the customer is investing in the vendor's technology because it has proven value and is far more economical than hiring a team. The longer-term investment pays off in the form of efficiency and productivity that will increase through continued use of the technology.

■ *Justify the cost.* The cost justification for the technology purchase comes down to simple economics. The formula for determining whether the investment is worthwhile is based on the organization's staff and skill set. Most software vendors have created their own return-on-investment (ROI) calculators as part of the sales process. Although these are a good starting point for determining whether the investment is worthwhile, they should not be taken at face value. One formula is to multiply the cost of hiring a team of software engineers (E) by the cost (C) of the software and divide that by the amount of time (T) required to realize ROI:

$$E \times C \,/\, T = ROI$$

To factor in the cost of hiring staff, keep in mind that the average salary for an application software engineer as of May 2008 was $85,430, with the highest 10 percent of this population earning more than $128,870.[17] When it comes to entry-level positions, the average starting salary offer for graduates with a bachelor's degree in computer science averaged $61,205 in 2009.[18]

■ *Evaluate the vendor.* Equally important as evaluating the software itself, if not more important, is to consider the health of the vendor that's selling it. Research the track records of the engineering team, the founder, and the executive team. You want to be sure that if you invest in the technology, the vendor will be around in the future to continue supporting you. This doesn't mean you should consider only the major software vendors when it comes to purchasing decisions. Many smaller, niche players can serve specific business needs that may be underserved by the larger players. In this instance, explore how the company sustains itself. Is it boot-strapped, funded by angel investors, or backed by established venture capitalists (VCs)? If so, who's behind the money, and what is their track record?

■ *Determine the product's actual version number.* You'll almost never find a version 1.0 of any product. The industry is well aware that the 1.0 label signifies that it's the first time the product is being released, which likely means that all the kinks have not been worked out. This is why you'll often find products that start with version 3.0. This doesn't mean the product is faulty or that a version 3.0 isn't just that. However, the version number is something to fully explore with regard to how the product will actually work after it's installed.

■ *Ask for customer references.* This may sound like a no-brainer given the time and costs associated with making a technology purchasing decision. Tread carefully down this path. Be leery of a vendor that claims to have impressive customer references, but the customers' corporate policies won't allow them to talk. Although this may be true from a public relations perspective, a satisfied customer should be available to speak to a prospect off the record. When you do get to that conversation with the customer, be sure to ask how long they've been using the product, if they receive a discount for being a reference, and the specifics of the product's best and worst features.

■ *Study industry analyst reports.* There are mixed reviews in the IT industry regarding the unbiased evaluations conducted by the analyst community. In many cases, analysts are a valuable resource to help companies determine their technology needs and which vendors are most capable of addressing them. They also provide in-depth market reports and forecasts. However, this community has a dark side that I'd argue is steeped in the analysts' preferences for vendors that subscribe to their services. The analyst community shouldn't be overlooked when it comes to evaluating technology, but you should ask if the vendors they are recommending to you are also their clients.

The Road Ahead

There's a lot to think about when technology is added to automobiles as well as other infrastructures and devices without a system of governance to ensure the quality of the products that are supposedly being enhanced. Specifically, I'm talking about IT governance. This includes a set of processes, policies, and best practices that are used to ensure that the best possible "glitch-free" software code is used as the foundation for nearly all our technology innovations.

Technology folks, especially those at the managerial level, are familiar with the term IT governance, which could help address many of these glitches. But to be clear, especially because you'll be reading more about it, I want to underscore that IT governance as it relates to glitches is not the same as compliance. I mention this because many people use these terms interchangeably. IT governance is complementary to the branch of technology called compliance that made its way into the spotlight as a result of the passing of the Sarbanes-Oxley Act of 2002.

Yet saying that IT governance is important and actually making it a reality are two very different things in many organizations. According to Lynn Cox, IT program manager at Ford Motor Company, "You have to educate the developers on the importance of IT governance. You can require mandatory training, but sometimes people will just show up and not pay attention. What you need to do is make it real for them. Share stories of real things that happen because of a lack of IT governance."[19]

Of course, Cox wouldn't disparage Ford's competition, but I would venture a guess that real-world stories and the role of IT governance are discussed more often at Ford these days in light of the Toyota situation.

Taking the Pulse on Healthcare IT

When it comes to healthcare and medicine, technology continues to play a critical role. Perhaps you were able to head off major dental surgery because your dentist took X-rays that revealed issues that had not yet risen to the surface. Or perhaps your child received x-rays when he fell off a swing. These common preventive measures can be quite helpful in quickly diagnosing breaks and fractures and avoiding potentially painful treatments down the line. Yet all of this adds up to a sevenfold increase in a person's average lifetime dose of diagnostic radiation since 1980.[20]

According to a series of articles on radiation that appeared in *The New York Times*, it has become woefully apparent that glitches are making their way into the very treatments that are supposed to save our lives. Included as an appendix in this book is one of the articles in the series, "Radiation Offers New Cures, and Ways to Do Harm."[21] It spells out the impact of these software glitches and their role in the deaths of several patients. A synopsis of the article follows.

Synopsis of the Article "Radiation Offers New Cures, and Ways to Do Harm"

Unless you really know your way around an oncology ward, you probably aren't familiar with a linear accelerator, or Linac. Essentially, this device is used to treat cancer patients by delivering a uniform dose of radiation to specifically treat a tumor. The beams that are delivered through the Linac destroy cancer cells while sparing the surrounding healthy tissue.

On the plus side, newer technology in Linac allows doctors to more accurately attack tumors and reduce certain mistakes. As with many computer-centric activities, there is a culturally accepted mind-set that because the process is computerized, it can't be wrong. Medicine is one area where that perception and the complexity curve collide. On the negative side, the complexity has created more opportunities for glitches to occur in terms of software flaws and faulty programming. These types of glitches impact the delivery of X-ray beams, as many patients have unfortunately discovered.

One of those patients was Scott Jerome-Parks. Before one of his radiation treatments for tongue cancer, Nina Kalach, the medical physicist responsible for overseeing the Linac, input the dosage and patient information into the software application. Kalach's input into the system would determine how much radiation the Linac would administer.

When Kalach tried to save her work, the computer froze. It's important to note that the software and Linac, provided by Varian Medical Systems, require three essential programming instructions that must be saved in sequence. The first step is the dose of radiation in the beam, the second is a digital image of the treatment area, and the third is the instructions that guide the multileaf collimator. This is a device within the Linac that is made up of individual "leaves" of high atomic numbered material that can move in and out of the path of a particle beam to block it from hitting unintended areas in the body with radiation.

Before the software program aborted, Kalach received an error message asking if she wanted to save her changes, and she replied yes. At that point, the system rebooted, and Kalach believed her changes were saved. Later that day, the computer crashed again and was again rebooted.

Six minutes after the second reboot, Jerome-Parks received the first of three radiation treatments. The next day he had another dose, as was the prescribed course of action. After the second dose, it was apparent from Jerome-Parks' physical condition that something had gone horribly wrong. His head and neck were swollen almost beyond recognition, and he was writhing in pain.

Nevertheless, Jerome-Parks underwent a third dose of radiation. Since the evidence was mounting that the patient was having more than an adverse reaction to the treatment, Kalach conducted a test on the technology and discovered that the multileaf collimator, which was supposed to focus the beam precisely on the tumor, was wide open. This meant that not only had Jerome-Parks' entire neck, from the base of his skull to his larynx, been mistakenly exposed, but he also had received seven times his prescribed dosage of radiation. Kalach also later learned that the software changes related to the patient's data were never saved before the computer crashed.

After his radiation treatments, Jerome-Parks continued to suffer from acute radiation toxicity. He could barely sleep or swallow, and he was hiccupping and vomiting. He needed a feeding tube and a constant stream of drugs and supplements. As his illness got worse, Jerome-Parks lost his hearing, eyesight, and balance. He died of acute radiation poisoning at the age of 43.

According to reports from the hospital that treated Jerome-Parks, similar system crashes "are not uncommon with the Varian software and these issues have been communicated to Varian on numerous occasions."

Varian's president and chief executive officer, Timothy Guertin, stated that the company had distributed new software with a fail-safe provision and also had warned customers to be especially careful when using their equipment.

Unfortunately, that updated software didn't arrive in time to help a woman who, several months later, was being radiated for cancer of the larynx. In this particular case, therapists tried to save a file on Varian equipment when the system's computer screen froze. Again, the multileaf collimator was wide open, and this particular patient received nearly six times her prescribed dose.

On the same day that warnings were issued to hospitals regarding Linac and its related software in light of the Jerome-Parks case, Alexandra Jn-Charles, 32, started radiation treatments for breast cancer. After 27 days of treatment, it was discovered that the Linac was missing a filter.

This resulted in Jn-Charles receiving three times the prescribed amount of radiation. It also resulted in a gaping wound in her chest that would not heal and eventually created a hole that exposed her ribs. After the radiation, Jn-Charles was repeatedly hospitalized for pain and had to live with the odor that was coming from the wound.

During this time, her cancer returned. Several months after her wound had finally healed, Jn-Charles passed away.

The stories of Scott Jerome-Parks and Alexandra Jn-Charles are not isolated incidents. A Philadelphia hospital gave the wrong radiation dose to more than 90 patients with prostate cancer and kept quiet about it. Meanwhile, in 2005, a Florida hospital disclosed that 77 brain cancer patients received 50 percent more radiation than prescribed because the linear accelerators had been programmed incorrectly for nearly a year. In another report about radiation missteps, one patient with stomach cancer was treated for prostate cancer, and another patient with brain cancer received radiation treatment intended for breast cancer.

Where Technology and Human Intellect Intersect

In fairness, it's important to note that not all of these mistakes were solely the result of technology. In several instances, human errors such as poor safety procedures or inadequate staffing and training also played a part.

What's more important to acknowledge is that the details of the radiation cases just discussed are shielded from public view by the government, doctors, and hospitals. Although privacy is a major concern, it seems that a bit more disclosure is needed, at least within the medical community, to help avoid these issues in the future. Moreover, no single agency oversees medical radiation. Therefore, accidents are underreported—if they are reported at all—because this isn't a requirement in all states. Realizing the potential problems associated with this issue, the New York State Legislature, along with the hospital industry, agreed in the 1980s to report medical mistakes. However, the identity of the institutions that made the mistakes remains cloaked.

Where is the line between human error at the hands of the Linac machine and at the hands of the keyboard when the software code is being written? Is it realistic to expect radiation physicists to become experts in computer programming, and vice versa? Just how much training goes into ensuring that hospital staff have mastered the use of the technology? How can software developers create more error-free programs?

These are complex issues and certainly can't be solved within the confines of this book. Besides, addressing these issues crosses many lines in technology, medicine, and government. However, I raise the questions to hopefully prompt discussions that will perhaps lead to awareness and action among those who can effect change. At the end of this chapter, I include suggestions for how we can more effectively address these issues as a society.

If you were wondering why I emphasize the importance of IT governance, these medical stories clearly underscore my reasoning. It is critical that software developers fully understand the impact of their efforts and the role that IT governance must play in the design and development of software.

I suspect the *The New York Times* report sparked many discussions at dinner tables and throughout the healthcare industry, many of which were centered on the likelihood of radiation poisoning happening to them or a loved one. According to Bill Klein, principal at Noblis Health Innovation's National Recall Center, "Over 48 percent of radiology recalls concerned software, with hardware problems following up at 38 percent."[22]

Noblis is a nonprofit science, technology, and strategy organization that is widely known for its RASMAS National Recall Center service. RASMAS helps healthcare facilities track recalled and defective supplies and equipment in 15 different product domains, including biologics, blood products, toys, food, pharmaceuticals, radiology products, and tissue.

What's a consumer to do? While the responsibility rests on the software developer, manufacturer, doctor, and technician, Klein suggests that patients ask their physicians about maintenance procedures, equipment operation, and staff accreditation. Additionally, patients can ask technicians and staff if there are established procedures to ensure that safety notices are dealt with quickly.

I also believe that patients and their families can use the power of technology for good. There's no reason why we can't stir a movement online to create a dedicated, comprehensive website that educates and informs the public about good and bad service at hospitals. If we can rank our experience at a hair salon or pizza parlor, why can't we take these social media technology tools a step further to warn people about potentially life-threatening experiences at local hospitals?

Lying by Omission

The issues at Toyota and those that *The New York Times* article brings to light are complex in that a variety of factors are associated with those tragic deaths and injuries. Aside from questioning the IT governance that was or wasn't in place at the software vendor, many other actions and people can be called into question. These include but are certainly not limited to the radiation physicists, hospital administrators, and government officials who are not demanding more stringent reporting of radiation poisoning.

Yet when it comes to full disclosure regarding these glitches, when is the boy crying wolf and unnecessarily alerting consumers to hazardous products, and when is it okay to delay notifying the public? Surely a more proactive approach to identifying and mitigating the risks associated with these glitches is the more strategic, cost-effective, and potentially life-saving course of action.

As IT and business professionals, we can no longer tolerate obfuscation of these glitches in the automotive and healthcare industries until they are discovered by consumers or required by law to become a matter of public record. We need to lead the charge to initiate the IT Governance Manifesto.

Not all healthcare glitches are as extreme as those outlined here. However, in an effort to improve the patient experience through technology, sometimes the best intentions go awry and wind up costing far more than anticipated.

Oregon: A Lesson Learned in Healthcare IT

In 2008, the Oregon Health Payment Plan was transitioning to a new $80 million IT system. Incidentally, the U.S. federal government is covering 90 percent of the costs of this system, which processes $200 million worth of claims each month.[23]

After two false starts, the system finally went online in December of that year. By September 2009, it had yet to accurately enroll and track residents who were eligible for services. For example, a report written in the morning might have indicated that a person was enrolled, while a report written in the afternoon said the opposite. Due to this glitch, the state of Oregon estimates that 2,800 new patients were "misplaced" over the course of a year, representing a loss of $9 million in annual revenue. Meanwhile, an Oregonian managed-care organization believes it has paid pharmacy and emergency room bills for patients that may not have been enrolled.

When the errors in the Oregon system dragged on for over nine months, the deputy director of Human Services hand-delivered a letter to contractor Electronic Data Systems (EDS). The letter demanded that the problems be fixed within 90 days, or the state could file suit. Twelve months of ongoing IT issues directly affected the bottom line for the state of Oregon, its healthcare providers, its residents, and the federal government. The actual cost is hard to quantify, because when they were asked about the financial impact, state officials and healthcare providers said they didn't know the answer.

Acknowledging the complexities involved, officials at the Oregon Department of Human Services said they expected glitches given the scope of the project.[24] I believe that somewhere in the middle of this mess lies a more balanced ground between the complexity of the system and the complacent attitude that errors will occur.

The issue in Oregon is yet another example illustrating that the scale of our infrastructures, the pace at which productivity must continue in IT, and the underlying economic factors are colliding despite our best efforts.

The issues at the Oregon Health Payment Plan are not unlike the IT projects that are currently under discussion or under way throughout the healthcare industry.

Throwing Good IT Dollars After Bad

While the Internet on the car dashboard is an obvious example, there are many instances in which technology is introduced into an infrastructure with the best intentions and worst execution.

Software errors are inevitable and glitches are unavoidable to a certain extent, but we should not invest more technology into a problem without a full understanding of the fundamental issues that initially caused the problem. Before any IT purchasing decisions are made, companies should undertake an extensive due diligence process.

The IT Governance Manifesto

Imagine if we could make consumers more aware of the potential risks lurking inside a product, system, or infrastructure. We've seen it with cigarettes and alcohol, but we have yet to see similar warnings applied to technology.

Companies would balk at the idea of having to publicly admit to shortcomings in their products. However, a third-party warning system is worth considering when it comes to products that affect our health and safety. I suggest this because I strongly believe and also gravely fear that we will see a rise in the number of software glitches before serious steps are taken to reduce their occurrence and the overall impact of glitches that manage to sneak past inspection.

The groundswell of personal health and safety issues due to software glitches will give rise to yet another dramatic consumer-driven market shift that will force change upon businesses of every size and in most industries.

The shift that's under way reminds me of President John F. Kennedy's Consumer Bill of Rights that was introduced in 1962.[25] Kennedy was responding to consumers demanding increased rights and legal protection against bad business practices. Kennedy's speech outlined six basic rights: The Right to Be Safe, The Right to Choose Freely, The Right to Be Heard, The Right to Be Informed, the Right to Education, and the Right to Service.

With this in mind, I firmly believe that consumers and businesses need to lobby government to pass legislation that mandates higher standards and establishes more concrete pass/fail criteria to eliminate the gray areas that so many products fall into. Product recalls are not enough.

This is why I'm proposing the IT Governance Manifesto. Making this vision a reality will require a cross-section of IT and business professionals, government agencies, and consumer advocacy groups that will join to accomplish the following:

- Lobby for new legislation that requires more stringent reporting of software glitches in matters of life and death.

- Impose fines on individuals and organizations responsible for software glitch cover-ups that put consumers' health and/or safety at risk.

- Require a specified level of IT governance at organizations that produce products that can directly affect a consumer's quality of life.

We can't sit idly by until the next auto or medical device manufacturer becomes the source of our personal tragedy or the subject of a government investigation. The expediency of the Motor Vehicle Safety Act of 2010 is evidence of how quickly the government can move when consumer safety is at stake. Therefore, there's no reason why we can't collectively start lobbying for the IT Governance Manifesto.

Endnotes

1. World's largest auto manufacturer rankings. The International Organization of Motor Vehicle Manufacturers. http://oica.net/wp-content/uploads/world-ranking-2008.pdf.

2. Toyota press release. Toyota Files Voluntary Safety Recall on Select Toyota Division Vehicles for Sticking Accelerator Pedal. http://pressroom.toyota.com/pr/tms/toyota/toyota-files-voluntary-safety-152979.aspx.

3. Toyota press release. Toyota Temporarily Suspends Sales of Selected Vehicles. http://pressroom.toyota.com/pr/tms/toyota/toyota-temporarily-suspends-sales-153126.aspx.

4. Toyota press release. Toyota Amends Recall on Potential Floor Mat Interference with Accelerator Pedal. http://pressroom.toyota.com/pr/tms/toyota/toyota-amends-recall-on-potential-153214.aspx.

5. AOL Autos. "Lexus Crash: An Avoidable Tragedy." Reilly Brennan. December 10, 2009. http://autos.aol.com/article/toyota-tragedy-saylor-family/.

6. U.S. Department of Transportation. NHTSA Launches Probe into Timeliness of Three Toyota Recalls. http://www.dot.gov/affairs/2010/dot2910.htm.

7. Toyota press release. Toyota Announces Voluntary Recall on 2010 Model-Year Prius and 2010 Lexus HS 250h Vehicles to Update ABS Software. http://pressroom.toyota.com/pr/tms/toyota-2010-prius-abs-recall-153614.aspx?ncid=12067.

8. Ibid.

9. National Highway Traffic and Safety Administration. United States Department of Transportation Responds to Third Toyota Recall. http://www.nhtsa.gov/PR/DOT-25-10.

10. United States House Committee on Oversight and Government Reform. "Toyota Gas Pedals: Is the Public at Risk?" February 24, 2010. http://oversight.house.gov/index.php?option=com_content&task=view&id=4798&Itemid=2.

11. Prepared Testimony of Akio Toyoda, President, Toyota Motor Corpora.
tion. Committee on Oversight and Government Reform. February 24,
2010. http://oversight.house.gov/images/stories/Hearings/
Committee_on_Oversight/2010/022410_Toyota/TESTIMONY-Toyoda.pdf.

12. U.S. House Energy and Commerce Committee. Motor Vehicle Safety
Act of 2010. April 29, 2010. http://energycommerce.house.gov/
Press_111/20100429/NHTSA.Motor.Vehicle.Safety.Act.Discussion.Draft.
Text.pdf.

13. National Highway Traffic Safety Administration. Statement from U.S.
Transportation Secretary Ray LaHood on Toyota's Agreement to Pay
Maximum Civil Penalty. http://www.nhtsa.gov/PR/DOT-71-10.

14. The number of automobile recalls has tripled: National Highway Traffic
Safety Administration databases. http://www-nrd.nhtsa.dot.gov/Cats/
index.aspx; Over 100 million lines of software code in luxury vehicles:
Frost and Sullivan. "Convergence in North American Auto Industry."
December 15, 2008.

15. iSuppli. Automotive Research Topical Report. "Internet in the Car: The
Future of In-Vehicle Connectivity." Q4 2009.

16. United States Department of Transportation. Distraction.gov: Official U.S.
Government Website for Distracted Driving. National Highway Traffic
Safety Administration. http://www.distraction.gov/stats-and-facts/.

17. U.S. Bureau of Labor Statistics. Occupational Employment Statistics
(OES) Survey Program. May 2008 National, State, Metropolitan, and
Nonmetropolitan Area Occupational Employment and Wage Estimates.

18. Winter 2010 Salary Survey. National Association of Colleges and
Employers.

19. Interview with Lynn Cox by Kathleen Keating. December 2009.

20. *New York Times* series: "The Radiation Boom. When Treatment Goes
Awry." "Radiation Offers New Cures, and Ways to Do Harm." Walt Bogdanich. January 23, 2010.

21. Ibid.

22. Interview: Bill Klein and Kathleen Keating. February 2010.

23. Oregon Department of Human Services, Division of Medical Assistance
Programs. January 11, 2010. http://www.oregon.gov/OHA/OHPB/
meetings/2010/care-or-1012.pdf.

24. Oregon Live. "Glitches Plague State Data System." August 7, 2009.

25. John F. Kennedy. Address to U.S. Congress. March 15, 1962. John F.
Kennedy Presidential Library and Museum.

CHAPTER 3

Cyber Terrorism and Other Hidden Threats

The subject of cyber terrorism is controversial and fear-inducing—and it's impossible to overlook in the context of this book's premise. Based on the research I conducted for this chapter, it's clear that governments and businesses all over the world have made reducing the threat of cyber terrorism and espionage a high priority.

Countless books, seminars, and conferences cover this topic. There are technology companies and government agencies solely focused on securing our IT infrastructures. Although security is certainly the main priority when it comes to protecting our nations and their citizens, the point of this chapter on cyber attacks, fraud, and overall threats to how we work and live is not to discuss security. Rather, I want to emphasize the importance of a sound infrastructure in supporting the extensive security that is required to keep countries, companies, and people safe.

The Threat Is Real

The experts have yet to agree on a concrete definition of cyber terrorism,[1] but suffice it to say that the threat of enemies using technology to cut off our water supplies, power grids, and access to finances is very real.

As quickly as we stockpile technology to fend off cyber attacks, the threat of those attacks becomes stronger. Currently more than 100 foreign intelligence agencies are trying to hack into the 15,000 U.S. government networks that are composed of more than seven million computers.[2] And the cost to defend these systems was more than a hundred million dollars during a six-month period in 2008.[3]

The enemy is no longer limited to being a foreign power. The enemy can be a high school hacker, online crime ring, or internal employee. The damage can be done in seconds but can take years to repair in terms of identifying the source, prosecuting the perpetrator, and reinforcing the compromised network. The issues around cyber defense will only grow in complexity as we continue to introduce more and new technologies into our networks. Figure 3.1 shows the increase in cyber security breaches from 2006 to 2008.[4]

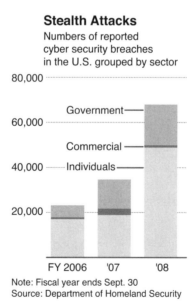

Figure 3.1   *Number of cyber security breaches in the U.S.*

Protecting the Power Grid

Imagine what it would be like to spend days without electric power due to a cyber attack. Picture the impact of losing power during an extremely hot or extremely cold day. Imagine the cascading effects of major cities such as New York, Hong Kong, London, Sydney, and Sao Paulo being in complete darkness, without traffic lights, home security, food supplies, and access to money. You may recall the Northeast Blackout of 2003, the largest ever to hit the United States, which left 55 million people throughout the United States and Canada without electricity. While al Qaeda terrorist groups tried to take credit for the blackout, an in-depth probe into the matter found that the blackout could have been prevented through better communication, equipment, and training.[5]

Regardless, protecting the power grid is top of mind for governments around the world. While not declaring that the U.S. electrical power grid has been attacked, the Department of Homeland Security has stated that the power grid is vulnerable to potentially disabling computer attacks.[6] This was in response to reports by the *Wall Street Journal* that Russian and Chinese cyber spies had made their way into the electrical grid to map the infrastructure and leave behind tools that could destroy parts of the infrastructure in the event of a crisis or a war with the U.S.[7]

There have also been reports regarding intrusions into the power grid throughout parts of Brazil in 2005, when three cities and tens of thousands of people were left without power. Another, more widespread attack supposedly happened on September 26, 2007 and affected more than three million people in dozens of cities over a two-day period.[8] However, the reports of these cyber attacks were largely disputed by the Brazilian government and its energy providers.[9]

To date, there has not been a full-fledged cyber attack on the U.S. grid, but experts believe it's just a matter of time.

According to director and chief economist Scott Borg of the U.S. Cyber Consequences Unit, the estimated damage from losing power for three months would be $700 billion.[10]

We need to be careful not to stir up paranoia about the grid's sustainability, but we must be mindful of the threats that exist. Preventing cyber attacks, or minimizing the effects should an enemy infiltrate a network, requires a deep understanding of the highly complex infrastructures that are currently in place.

The Million-Dollar-a-Day Upgrade

Although it wasn't caused by a cyber attack, the technology incident at the Hatch nuclear power plant near Baxley, Georgia is worth addressing. In March 2008, an engineer who was connected to the plant's network decided to install what he thought was a simple software upgrade on his own computer. Since he was connected to the network, the upgrade inadvertently brought down the entire system for 48 hours in an automatic, unplanned shutdown. Such a shutdown, which was required at Hatch due to federal protocol, forces utilities to purchase power from other parts of the grid—to the tune of $1 million a day.[11]

The complexities of the infrastructure were unknown to the engineer because of the differing expertise in the organization among IT staff and those responsible for the plant's industrial control system (ICS). The ICS is the technology brain that enables the delivery of power to customers. It was impossible for the engineer to fully understand how the ICS intersects with the computer network, nor would that knowledge ever be a job requirement. This is an example of where the infrastructure would have benefited from having certain controls and mechanisms in place to prevent the software upgrade. And it underscores the importance of sound IT.

According to Joe Weiss, professional engineer and certified information security manager at Applied Control Systems, a consultancy specializing in optimizing and securing ICS, "The

IT staff can cause an outage even while following existing IT policies [because they are] unaware of ICS issues."[12] As the author of *Protecting Industrial Control Systems from Electronic Threats*,[13] Weiss also commented on the threat of terrorists attacking the electric power grid: "The current systems were not designed with awareness of cyber threats, regardless of whether they are deliberate or accidental. Control systems are in the formative stage for cyber security—arguably where IT was ten years ago. It will likely be another five to ten years before we start to design new control systems with security as part of the initial design."

We may fundamentally grasp that our electrical grids, local power suppliers, and government agencies require far more sophisticated technology on the back end, yet the complexities that make those systems run are genius. Figure 3.2 shows the control system at an energy provider and just how complex the infrastructure can be. And this is one of the simplest depictions of it.

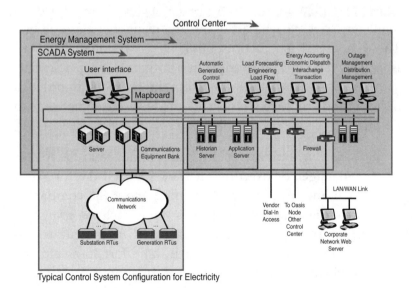

Figure 3.2   *Control system configuration for electricity*[14]

To be more proactive about the looming threat of porous infrastructures at power plants, Weiss suggests cross-disciplinary training between IT and industrial control systems personnel on equipment and best practices. He also believes that "senior management must provide budget, directive, and get all stakeholders involved in addressing cyber security."

Building a Sound Employee Infrastructure

Weiss' recommendations can be applied to nearly every industry and to nearly every facet of the organization. It's up to the organization to create a culture where security is a priority by making it top of mind for every employee. Along these lines, it would be worth the investment to ensure that each employee has a better understanding of the bigger picture.

We've talked about cross-training developers to better manage the COBOL issue, and in our everyday dialog with each other, we stress the importance of managing up. When it comes to IT planning, we're advised to include line-of-business managers so that each part of the organization is represented. These are great best practices. But I believe we could all benefit from less talking and more action to gain a deeper understanding of each other's roles across the company in order to build a solid employee infrastructure. Here are some ways to do this:

- *Shadowing:* Employees can better understand the role of a manager or executive if they spend a day or week attending meetings and learning about the company's operations. Many companies have such programs in place, but they are often provided for executives-in-training or are too scripted in an effort to shield the employee from confidential information. Confidentiality notwithstanding, the real benefits of a shadow program come when an employee is exposed to real business issues.

- *Peer-to-peer job exchange:* These can be short- or long-term assignments so that employees gain a better perspective of how a peer in a different part of the company contributes to his or her team and the organization as a whole. Similar programs exist in organizations where employees swap the same role in a different country or state. These exchange programs are valuable, yet a peer-to-peer program across different departments can help create a well-rounded view of the company for the employees.

- *Executives on the shop floor:* When an executive visits a site location, days or even weeks of planning go into the preparation for the internal inspection. I'd argue that a good chunk of that time would be better allocated to making sure the customers are pleased. When executives visit different facilities, there shouldn't be any fanfare about their arrival, nor should their presence strike fear into employees. Executives would be well served if they spent a few hours or days getting a solid grasp on the organization's inner workings by parking themselves alongside the employees who are making the products.

Bank Robbers Can Telecommute

Although most of our battles are fought face-to-face, cyber attacks are arguably more alarming, because they subtly steal our identities and slowly drain our pockets. One of the biggest cyber heists to date happened in November 2008. A transnational crime organization withdrew over $9 million in less than 12 hours from 2,100 RBS WorldPay ATMs in 280 cities throughout the U.S., Russia, Ukraine, Estonia, Italy, Japan, and Canada. Along with the money, the hackers also made off with financial data on 1.5 million customers and the social security numbers of 1.1 million customers.[15]

The RBS WorldPay bank robberies were extensive due to the speed of the transactions. These speeds are widely recorded in increments of transactions per minute, per second, and per millisecond. To better understand the speed of transactions in our digital world, more than 3.7 billion standardized financial messages were exchanged in December 2009 alone, according to the Society for Worldwide Interbank Financial Telecommunication (SWIFT). Figure 3.3 shows financial transactions for 2009 according to SWIFT.

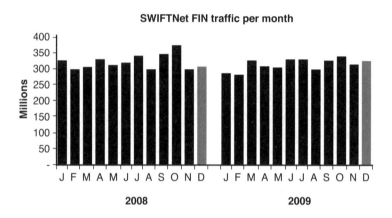

SWIFTNet FIN traffic per month

Figure 3.3   *Record of executed financial transactions according to SWIFT*

By the time the RBS WorldPay cyber bank robbers were halted, they had already done a significant amount of damage.[16] The victim of a sophisticated hacker ring, RBS WorldPay could just as easily have been another multinational financial organization or perhaps the bank that handles your finances.

It's All Fun and Games Until…

Moving from a direct hit on a bank to a more subtle form of attack on consumers is very likely in the wildly popular massively multiplayer online game (MMOG) market. Bringing together hundreds of thousands of players simultaneously in an online world escalates the number of transactions in the infrastructure that need to be properly managed. With that many players online at the same time, there is bound to be at least one unscrupulous participant who has more in mind than a harmless round of World of Warcraft. A few minutes in the virtual world could do serious damage to unsuspecting consumers in terms of identity theft and spreading computer viruses to those who are online to simply play a game.

In some instances, the transaction speeds are barely perceptible because they come pretty darn close to breaking the speed of light. Like the RBS WorldPay heist, the perpetrators in MMOG typically aren't caught until after they've done a world of harm.

Going beyond the MMOG example, the rapid pace of technology challenges businesses in nearly every industry to uncover the cause-and-effect relationships among seemingly disparate events or minute market changes that occur in milliseconds yet can have significant business impact.

This is especially critical when you consider that approximately 1.8 billion people around the world are connected to the Internet, according to Internet World Stats. Many of them rely on it for personal banking, self-employment, filling prescriptions, and nearly any other transaction that used to be conducted face-to-face. Figure 3.4 shows Internet usage by country.

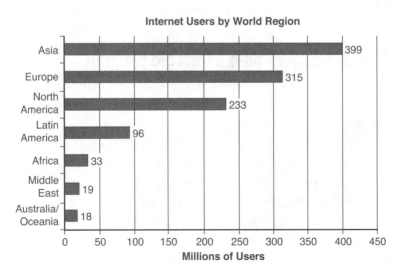

Figure 3.4   *Internet users by world region as of 2009*[17]

Spotting trends that represent threats and being able to get ahead of them or stem them as they happen requires a balance between creating a solid IT foundation and reinforcing it through the proper security technologies.

Does this mean that we should never log on again, or that we should return to the good old days of asking strangers for directions and rushing home to make sure we don't miss that landline telephone call? Certainly not. After all, we have come too far too fast to disregard the amazing IT industry and profit center that we have collectively created.

When we read about these cyber attacks and inadvertent system failures, we might be tempted to say "Just fix it." Since the majority of our daily interactions with technology are relatively simple, it's easy to take the point-and-click experience for granted. It is far more difficult on the part of the engineer, architect, or developer to make the user experience simple. Although turning on a light, powering down a computer, and accessing your 401k online may be simple actions you do on a regular basis, they require thousands if not millions of lines of code behind the scenes to make them happen. From an IT perspective, those activities are important and complex but are not on the same level as the technology that is required to run and protect our governments and global businesses.

The IT Infrastructure as a Strategic Weapon

In this global economy, we have to ask, "If business doesn't stop at the border, why should our computers?" This can be a matter of national as well as international safety.

In September 2009, police in northwest England stopped Johnny "Mad Dog" Adair on the road because they believed he was a suspicious character, yet they couldn't recall why his face was familiar. When the Police National Computer didn't reveal any previous offenses or outstanding warrants, the officers let him go. Still uneasy, the officers followed their gut instinct and decided to conduct a more thorough search on

Adair when they returned to the station. The results showed that he was convicted of assaulting his wife in 2005.

If the Police National Computer had been fully integrated with the criminal database in Northern Ireland, the officers would have been alerted to the fact that Adair was also a convicted terrorist and former commander in the terrorist group known as the Ulster Freedom Fighters.

The incompatibilities among the computer systems and an accompanying glitch were making hundreds of convicted terrorists virtually invisible to the British police. These issues were compounded by the fact that many of these terrorists had moved from Northern Ireland to England, Scotland, and Wales.[18]

The Impact of an Aging Infrastructure

We can well imagine the impact of losing our power supply and can empathize with the frustration of the police in northwest England. Yet fortifying the systems that make it possible to turn on the lights in our homes and keep computers running in the office is not as simple as bolting on additional security mechanisms or simply fusing various sources of information.

The infrastructures that are in place are highly complex, have evolved over decades, and consist of different software applications. Many of those applications are proprietary and have been customized to meet the company's specific business needs and the customers it supports. These circumstances are not unlike those at many companies across various industries.

To illustrate this point using an analogy, think about the IT infrastructure as the foundation of a house. As you start to build on top of that foundation with beams, floors, plumbing, wiring, and the like, you need to be sure that your architects have designed the right plans and that your builders are following those plans using the right tools. Everybody involved must follow the mandated codes so that you are creating a sound structure that will endure for decades, if not a century and beyond. If any mistakes are made in how the concrete was mixed and poured, or cracks appear over time, the entire structure will eventually break down. When IT architects mapped out infrastructures decades ago, they couldn't have imagined today's fully digital and connected world, where an invisible enemy can infiltrate through a computer.

Adding new security tools or complex enterprise software today is like building an addition onto your house. It needs to be carefully included as an extension to the foundation, without disrupting any of the plumbing or wiring. If the technology doesn't map to the larger architectural strategy, parts of the system can break down, leaving the company more vulnerable to attack.

Introducing New Technologies into Legacy Infrastructures

Taking advantage of newer technologies, including security tools and devices, without compromising the value of the existing infrastructure is a challenge that can deliver significant benefits if approached and executed properly. Here are some recommendations for ensuring a smoother integration with newer technologies:

- *Map the infrastructure.* Before you add any technology to the infrastructure, be sure you have a comprehensive and current view of the entire architecture, as well as how new technology will impact existing systems. This should include simulations of the domino effect should a new piece of technology be put into the infrastructure.

- *Take an incremental approach.* Resist the temptation to roll out new technology across the entire organization. First, test it privately among your internal development team, and be sure to test it under the worst possible circumstances. From there, try it with smaller teams in the company. At each stage, make sure you gather feedback, and make adjustments accordingly before the technology advances to the next team. This approach should be a critical part of the planning efforts so that realistic dead-lines are set and met.

- *Learn to compromise.* Despite aggressive and well-executed efforts, you won't be able to integrate every piece of your existing technology with the newer offer-ings. If the architectural strategy is well mapped out in advance of any development or integration work, this will not be a surprise. While you'll try to migrate as much technology as possible, you should also build in plans from a staffing and budgeting perspective to rewrite the code in the newer environment.

- *Know when to leave well enough alone.* Given fluctuations in staffing and long-term investments in technology, the reality is that you simply won't fully understand certain applications. You will know what they do and how they work to help the business, but you will not always know exactly what makes them tick from a software code perspective. If it's a business-critical application, such as one that makes sure the electricity goes from the power supplier to the home, you may not need to know every line of code if the application is running properly. In this instance, the risk of compromising the infrastructure by opening the application far outweighs the need to sate curiosity.

Preventing a Digital Pearl Harbor

Dr. Jim Lewis is the director of the Center for Strategic and International Studies (CSIS) and one of the world's most respected experts on cyber terrorism. One of Lewis' more recent reports on the subject was the "Report of the CSIS Com-mission on Cybersecurity for the 44th Presidency."[19] This report is a comprehensive review of the current state of cyber terrorism that was prepared in December 2008 for then-Presi-dent-elect Barack Obama.

In February 2010, Dr. Lewis testified before the Senate Commerce Committee and brought to light the impact of cyber crime on a day-to-day basis. In his testimony, Lewis said, "We talk about cyber attack and cyber war when we really should be saying cyber espionage and cyber crime. Espionage and crime are not acts of war. They are, however, daily occurrences on the Internet, with the U.S. being the chief victim, and they have become a major source of harm to national security. The greatest damage to the U.S. comes from espionage, including economic espionage. We have lost more as a nation to espionage than at any time since the 1940s. The damage is usually not visible, but, of course, the whole purpose of espionage is not to be detected."[20]

While reading some of Lewis' research in preparation for the interview with him,[21] I was reminded of the discussions from the 1990s about the threat of a digital Pearl Harbor and how relevant that catchphrase still is today.

Lewis shared as much as he could about the state of our national security infrastructure without compromising the safety of our country. What follows is an excerpted Q&A from my interview with Lewis:

Q. What can we do better to reduce the threat of cyber terrorism?

A. We need to get more people and more companies to adopt the better technologies that will make us more secure. To do this, we need to better define the incentives that will advance the adoption of better technology. We also need to work with other governments so that we are all in agreement with the rules of the road when it comes to cyberspace.

It used to be that the U.S. was by far the dominant force in technology, and while it is still the leader, other countries have come to the forefront, and we are taking advantage of those technologies as well. We learned to work with other countries in that regard. Now we need to learn to work with other governments so that we are all in agreement on how we can better respond to threats in cyberspace.

Q. We've come so far in technology over the past few decades, so what is it about the threat of cyber attacks that makes conquering them so elusive?

A. While we have come very far in all areas of technology, including our defense against cyber attacks, we're not quite there yet. It's a maturity issue. You have to remember that while we just formally celebrated the 40th anniversary of the Internet, the commercial Internet that the majority of us know and use is only about 15 years old.

Just like we saw with the first airplanes and automobiles, we had to be working with them for a longer period of time to advance them and eliminate their issues as each new model is developed. The same can be said for new technologies and applications. We will see better versions of applications down the road, but it's an iterative process. We continue to improve it, and we're certainly getting closer to our goals.

Q. What can we do as citizens to help curb the threat of cyber terrorism?

A. A lot of it comes down to education and awareness. Education is definitely one way of making people more aware. For example, I gave a talk a few years back, and I asked the audience how many of them had been to the Beijing Olympics, and a good amount of people raised their hands. The next question I asked was how many of them brought their BlackBerrys with them when they were at the Olympics, and a fair amount of hands went up. Then I asked how many were aware that the Chinese government was monitoring their BlackBerry while they were in the country. The surprised look on their faces pretty much gave me my answer about the level of awareness of how the Internet works in countries outside the U.S.

In the United States, we have free access to any information on the Internet, so we just assume this is the way it is overseas. And China is not the only country that monitors its citizens on the Internet. So there's still a lot of work to be done to figure out the rules of the road with cyber usage in different countries as it relates to preventing cyber attacks.

Q. Where does IT governance fit into the picture with regard to protecting us against cyber attacks?

A. IT governance is critical to protecting us against cyber attacks. You have to think about IT governance like wearing a seatbelt every time you get behind the wheel. In order for the seat belt to be effective, you have to not only wear it, it also has to be enforced by the law. It's the IT governance process that will create better and more secure environments. There will also be things that technology can't do, and that is why we need to work more closely with governments to address all of the security issues.

Lewis is a realist when it comes to advising about cyber attacks. As he so accurately pointed out, although we can't solve every issue through technology, IT governance certainly plays a critical role. Lewis is not the only industry luminary to use the seat belt analogy, as you'll see in a future chapter. I've included it twice in the book because it's a direct quote from two industry experts that helps illustrate the relevance and role of IT governance to a broader audience. In addition, I believe this analogy eloquently raises the issue that perhaps IT governance should be mandated by law in certain high-risk, high-visibility situations.

Great Strides, Yet Miles to Go

On November 17, 2009, Steven R. Chabinsky, deputy assistant director of the Cyber Division of the United States Federal Bureau of Investigation (FBI), testified at a Congressional hearing. Chabinsky provided an overview of how the FBI's anti-cyber crime task force works, along with its latest accomplishments.

In a transcript from the session, Chabinsky shared many positive milestones of the agency's work. Within the context of the update, Chabinsky was quoted as saying, "...a compelling act of terror in cyberspace could take advantage of a limited window of opportunity to access and then destroy portions of our networked infrastructure." He went on to say, "...we, as a nation, continue to deploy new technologies without having in place sufficient hardware or software assurance schemes or sufficient security processes that extend through the entire life cycle of our networks."[22]

Earlier that year, similar warnings and recommendations were shared at the Conference on International Police Cooperation Against Cyber Crime held in New Delhi. During the conference, Senior Cabinet Secretary K. M. Chandrasekhar warned, "There could be attacks on critical infrastructure such as telecommunications, power distribution, transportation, financial services, essential public utility services, and others."[23] Certainly, government leaders throughout the world echo these sentiments.

A Global IT Governance Council

It's clear that none of us is 100 percent safe from a cyber attack or cyber crime, regardless of how sophisticated and encrypted our systems are. However, we can get much closer to that 100 percent range than we currently are.

The U.S. government is hard at work addressing these issues and assembling forces across its various agencies and the private sector to use technology to thwart attacks. Augmenting these efforts could be the Global IT Governance Council, which would work in concert with businesses, government agencies, and existing security councils to establish more concrete guidelines and policies to protect the infrastructure. More specifically, the council would have the following goals:

- Work with government leaders throughout the world to establish criteria for creating more solid IT infrastructures through governance to protect countries from cyber attacks, cyber crime, and espionage.

- Establish and enforce consistent penalties and fines across the globe against the perpetrators of cyber crimes and cyber attacks.

- Create a warning system to alert the online community when they are about to enter a website that doesn't meet minimum security requirements as determined by the Global IT Governance Council.

- Provide more education for citizens on how to better protect against cyber crime. This would include working with state and local governments to offer free workshops for adults, as well as coordinating with educators to include courses on preventing cyber attacks as part of the high school curriculum.

- Serve as an expert resource that organizations could freely consult for unbiased third-party advice and best practices related to protecting the infrastructure.

Endnotes

1. Harvard Law Record. "What is cyberterrorism? Even experts can't agree." Victoria Baranetsky. November 5, 2009. http://www.hlrecord. org/news/what-is-cyberterrorism-even-experts-can-t-agree-1.861186.

2. Center for Strategic and International Studies. Speech on Cyber Security at the Center for Strategic and International Studies. Delivered by Deputy Secretary of Defense William J. Lynn. June 15, 2009. http://www.defense.gov/speeches/speech.aspx?speechid=1365.

3. Ibid.

4. United States Department of Homeland Security.

5. Report to the U.S.-Canada Power System Outage Task Force. "The August 14, 2003 Blackout One Year Later: Actions Taken in the United States and Canada to Reduce Blackout Risk." Natural Resources Canada, The United States Department of Energy. August 13, 2004.

6. Reuters. "Has Power Grid Been Hacked? U.S. Won't Say." Steve Holland and Randall Mikkelsen. April 8, 2009.

7. *Wall Street Journal*. "Electricity Grid in U.S. Penetrated by Spies." Siobhan Gorman. April 8, 2009.

8. *60 Minutes*. CBS Television. "Cyberwar: Sabotaging the System." November 8, 2009.

9. *Wired*. "Brazilian Blackout Traced to Sooty Insulators, Not Hackers." Marcelo Soares. November 9, 2009.

10. CNN.com. "Staged cyber attack reveals vulnerability in power grid." http://edition.cnn.com/2007/US/09/26/power.at.risk/index.html.

11. *Washington Post*. "Cyber Incident Blamed for Nuclear Power Plant Shutdown." Brian Krebs. June 5, 2008. http://waterfallsecurity.com/wp-content/uploads/2009/11/CyberIncidentBlamedForNuclearPower-PlantShutdownJune08.pdf.

12. Interview with Joe Weiss by Barbara McGovern. February 2010.

13. *Protecting Industrial Control Systems from Electronic Threats*. Joseph Weiss. Momentum Press, 2010. ISBN: 978-1-60650-197-9.

14. Control System Configuration for Electricity. "Roadmap to Secure Control Systems in the Energy Sector." Sponsored by the United States Department of Energy and the United States Department of Homeland Security. Prepared by Energetics Incorporated.

15. *Washington Post*. "Eight Indicted in $9M RBS WorldPay Heist." Brian Krebs. November 10, 2009. http://voices.washingtonpost.com/security-fix/2009/11/eight_indicted_in_9m_rbs_world.html.

16. RBS WorldBank: United States of America Versus Viktok Pleschuk, Sergei Tsurikov, Hacker 3, Oleg Covelin, Igor Grudijev, Ronald Tsoi, Evelin Tsoi, and Mihhail Jevgenov. United States District Court for the Northern

District of Georgia, Atlanta Division. November 10, 2009. http://voices. washingtonpost.com/securityfix/RBSIndictment.pdf.

17. Internet World Stats. http://www.internetworldstats.com/stats.htm.

18. Times Online. "Computer Glitch Leaves Ulster Terrorists Invisible." Sean O'Neill. September 14, 2009. http://www.timesonline.co.uk/tol/news/ uk/crime/article6832946.ece.

19. "Securing Cyberspace for the 44th Presidency." A report of the CSIS Commission. December 2008. Center for Strategic and International Studies. http://csis.org/files/media/csis/pubs/081208_securingcyberspace_44. pdf.

20. U.S. Senate Committee on Commerce, Science, and Transportation Hearings. "Cybersecurity: Next Steps to Protect Our Critical Infrastructure." Dr. James Lewis. February 23, 2010.

21. Interview with Dr. Jim Lewis by Jeff Papows. February 2010.

22. U.S. Senate Judiciary Committee Subcommittee on Terrorism and Homeland Security at a hearing titled "Cybersecurity: Preventing Terrorist Attacks and Protecting Privacy Rights in Cyberspace." Steven R. Chabinsky. November 17, 2009. http://judiciary.senate.gov/pdf/ 11-17-09%20New%20Chabinsky%20Testimony.pdf.

23. Conference on International Police Cooperation Against Cyber Crime, held in New Delhi. March 26, 2009. Central Bureau of Investigation. http://cbi.nic.in/speech/dcbi_cybercrime_20090326.php.

CHAPTER 4

Dealing with Everyday Glitches

Most IT glitches are identified and addressed quickly. Still others can take days or even weeks before they're repaired. On the surface, these system errors are, at a minimum, annoyances that reflect an oversight or a shortcut in the software design. In many cases it may not be a shortcut at all, but a reflection of the growing complexity of the infrastructure.

The results of an IBM Global CEO study released in 2010 further indicate that the IT infrastructure will continue to become more complicated. The survey participants included more than 1,500 CEOs, general managers, and government officials from 60 countries spanning 33 industries. While eight in ten of the survey participants expect the complexity of the IT infrastructure to increase, only 49 percent believe that their companies are prepared to handle it.[1]

Adding to this is the fact that we continue to breathe in data like it's air. The current size of the world's digital content is equivalent to all the information that could be stored on 75 billion Apple iPads, or the amount that would be generated by everyone in the world posting messages on the microblogging site Twitter continuously for a century.[2]

All of these factors contribute to unintentional yet insidious glitches. This chapter looks at how these glitches make their way into the infrastructure and what we can do to more effectively manage the processes that allow them to proliferate.

The Evolving IT Infrastructure

Keeping up with trends and determining what's hype and what's real are only part of the typical ten-hour workday in the IT industry. The biggest challenges come from sustaining the infrastructure that fuels the business. To put the complexity of the evolving IT infrastructure in perspective, take a closer look at Figure 4.1. It maps the types of tools, software languages, and embedded systems within the context of Internet services.[3]

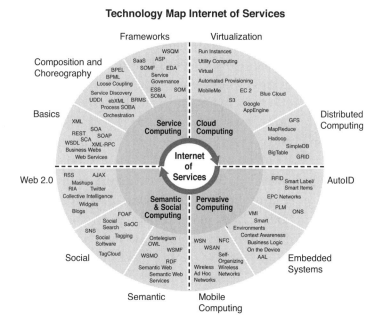

Figure 4.1 *Technology map of Internet services*

Within each slice of the pie are hundreds of potential technology products that can be added to the infrastructure. As we continue to innovate in the pursuit of productivity, we also need to properly manage that innovation so that we are not draining our physical and intellectual IT resources.

However, building more efficient business models through the IT infrastructure is not an easy feat. In some instances, the risks outweigh the rewards because you don't just have to reinforce your infrastructure. You also have to be mindful of the infrastructures managed by the companies you're doing business with online.

Increasingly complex infrastructures, a rise in the amount of data we continue to consume, and the growth of online collaboration and commerce are contributing to the creation of these unintentional yet insidious glitches.

These glitches aren't headline news, but they do stall productivity. They are the everyday hiccups that cause us to reboot our computers, unnecessarily spend time on customer support lines alerting staff to issues, and basically make us think twice about doing business again with certain vendors.

Breaking down some of the complexities of the infrastructure is a matter of stepping back and understanding how we've accumulated so much technology. Three critical factors contribute to this:

- The availability of cheap and powerful processors
- Reduced costs through outsourcing
- Easier access to enterprise software

The Availability of Cheap and Powerful Processors

A walk around any appliance store is evidence of how we've been able to add more technology into our homes. We've souped up our washers and dryers to make them more energy-efficient. Our coffee pots automatically know to start brewing at the same time our light-sensitive digital alarm clocks help us start the day. And our refrigerators are programmed to adjust to temperature fluctuations if their doors are continually opened and closed, as is the case when my kids are home. Although all these innovations certainly make our lives easier, they also illustrate just how much technology is entrenched in every action and interaction.

As IBM's Software Group Senior Vice President, Steve Mills, told me during our interview for this book, "There are one billion transistors for each person on the planet. We're seeing an almost cosmic-like expansion where intelligence is everywhere. Everything will become instrumented, including supply chains, health care networks, cities, and even natural systems like rivers."[4]

As Mills pointed out, we've been putting intelligence into products and devices for decades. We've been able to do this because the price of 64-bit processors has dropped significantly, making them easier and less expensive to embed in products.

To put this in perspective, the speed of the processor determines how fast the computer or device will process information. This speaks directly to Moore's Law, which was published in 1965. It states that the number of transistors on a chip will double about every two years.[5] Since the first 64-bit processor was introduced in 1992,[6] the power continues to accelerate with each iteration. Since many of our consumer devices don't require more than 64-bit processors to deliver high-end features, this explains the price drop and why the latest appliances and devices are now fully loaded.

Whether or not you subscribe to Moore's Law, it's impossible to overlook the 2010 introduction of the Itanium line processors by Intel, the world leader in silicon innovation.[7] The world's fastest processors allow us to process information and download larger, multimedia-rich files and applications at speeds never before possible while more efficiently balancing the consumption of energy. Making data and digital files that much more accessible to an increasing number of connected users increases our reliance on technology. The more dependent we are on technology, the more technology we need. To take advantage of this processing power without slowing down our applications or allowing glitches to quickly sneak past inspection comes down to the health of the IT infrastructure itself.

Reduced Costs Through Outsourcing

The rise of outsourcing for software development activities will remain a controversial topic for the foreseeable future. On paper, it appears to be a cost-effective way to take advantage of overseas IT skills, yet the results have been mixed. The biggest disconnect has been in justifying the cost savings in comparison to the quality of service delivered. Lower quality software cook is often rife with glitches.

However, the benefits of outsourcing can be reaped if both the client and service provider take the right approach. Elizabeth Grealy, CEO and cofounder of Grealy Globalization Enterprises, a Boston, Massachusetts consulting firm specializing in ensuring successful outsourcing engagements, shared with me some of these critical success factors:[8]

- *Top-level support.* Make sure the senior management team, including the CIO and CEO, are fully vested in the success of the outsourcing program, from vendor selection through the ongoing progression of a mutually beneficial relationship with the outsourcing firm.

- *Experienced management team.* The maturity and discipline of the management team—of both the client and the service provider—are directly tied to the cost savings and benefits that can be gained. As Grealy pointed out, "When you have a team sitting outside your office, you can pull them in for a quick meeting or for fast turnaround on a project. With outsourcing, you need to have vision and be proactive in the way that the project is being managed and executed, because you are working with a remote team. Essential to a successful outsourcing experience is the need for structure, including formalized requirements, scope, communication, and development processes and issues management."

- *Accurate assessment of what can be outsourced.* Distinguish between core and noncore activities to determine which projects should be outsourced. The core activities are considered the company's intellectual property and are the primary revenue-generating functions that are best handled by the company itself.

- *Consult with reputable outsourcing experts.* It's worth the investment to cultivate a relationship with a globalization expert if you are interested in an outsourcing program. In evaluating experts, be sure they can help define the business requirements, will outline the infrastructure for an outsourcing program, and will help steer the efforts that result in successful engagements. Additionally, they should be conversant in relevant software languages and development methodologies and understand the nuances of your industry.

- *Consider the following factors in the decision process:*
  - The team's experience with industry and technology and their education levels
  - Experience and history of the service provider
  - Potential language barriers for customer-facing assignments
  - Knowledge of local laws and the ability to enforce contractual agreements
  - The physical infrastructure of the outsourcer's offices, including building security, access to the office through modernized roadways, and stable electricity
  - The IT infrastructure of the outsourcer's offices, including networks and disaster recovery plans
  - Geopolitical status of the country and the service provider
- *Leave nothing to chance.* Be extremely detailed and clear in outlining the scope of work, roles and responsibilities, deliverables, and service level agreements.
- *Establish governance processes and policies around the following:*
  - Security and confidentiality standards
  - Staff reporting structure
  - Legal agreements including noncompete clauses

- Auditing to ensure adherence to corporate and regulatory requirements

- *Try before you buy.* If you are planning to outsource more sophisticated software development efforts, consider having a prototype developed by the proposed team to validate their development skills and their ability to apply those skills to your code.

- *Be prepared for turnover.* It's no secret that turnover rates at some outsourcing firms can be high. While you can't force an employee to stay, you can build contingencies and incentives into the contract. These hold the outsourcer responsible for meeting the deadline with a quality product and reward the outsourcer at the project's completion.

- *Take an incremental approach.* Allocate appropriate time for proper knowledge transfer. As with any major IT effort with a new team, you should take an incremental approach to ensure the work's quality and consistency.

- *View outsourcing as a partnership.* A stronger relationship with the service provider is established through trust in every exchange and business transaction. From a more tactical point of view, it's important to invest in team-building exercises, employee exchange programs, and staggered schedules to ensure live conversations among the integrated team. Fostering an environment where there is trust and the outsourcing team feels like part of your organization is a critical part of reducing turnover, improving productivity, and raising the quality of product that's delivered.

Significant benefits can be gained through outsourcing. According to Grealy, "If approached and managed properly, companies can save between 20 and 30 percent annually through outsourcing."

Creating sound infrastructures isn't solely an issue of internal versus external employees. The more hands that are involved in developing software, the greater the risk of vulnerability and compromises in the end product if the organization lacks agreed-upon standards and approaches. Using technology to automate part of the software development processes and flag potential issues before they get too far down the line can also improve the overall quality of the code, regardless of whose hands are at the keyboard.

Easier Access to Enterprise Software

The software as a service model has enabled more companies to take advantage of higher-end features and functions without needing to add headcount to manage the software. Although a third party owns and manages the software, the technology itself still intersects with your infrastructure through the employee's computer. This can potentially add a level of risk due to greater exposure of your infrastructure.

Along with the subscription-based software model is the ability for companies to easily download new versions of enterprise software that are made available through the vendor. Although upgrades can boost productivity, they also add to the infrastructure if no process is in place to ensure that older versions are phased out properly.

Two additional factors are driving up the expansion of technology in a company and the complexity of managing it:

- Healthy curiosity among IT professionals
- A mismatch between technology and business

Healthy Curiosity Among IT Professionals

IT professionals tend to be curious about the latest development tools, applications, and programming languages. One of the roles of an IT professional is to closely watch and test the latest technology offerings.

However, avoiding introducing rogue technology into the company is a two-step process that requires a system of checks and balances. It takes into account people and processes as well as the overall business value the technology brings to the company.

The first step of avoiding this behavior is using a road map that is aligned with the company's business direction. Realistically, a clear vision should account for the next 24 months. To stay on course with that road map, you should ask two questions before you purchase or download any technology:

- Does it benefit the organization economically and strategically?

- Can we easily build it ourselves?

The second step is trusting that your senior-level IT professionals have the experience to answer those two questions. Along with their effective people-management skills comes the need to institute IT processes that will prohibit unauthorized technology from making its way into the company. Although leadership, trust, and experience are valuable assets, the organization also must put controls in place that prevent technology from being used if it doesn't reflect the larger business goals or could disrupt the company's day-to-day operations.

In the context of healthy curiosity, it would be impossible to overlook the contributions of the open source community, because open source often helps solve business challenges. However, before you decide to allow open source software into your infrastructure, be sure that you have a dedicated team internally to manage it and participate in the advancement of the community. Before selecting an open source solution and purchasing a service plan, be sure that the vendor behind it has a dedicated team for service and support. That way, you won't rely on unknown, external resources for the latest patches, upgrades, and answers to questions.

A Mismatch Between Technology and Business

Even after a thorough product evaluation, a mismatch can occur between the technology's features and its ability to help support business goals. This can happen for several reasons, all of which can interrupt the flow of business. Two of the more common issues are skills and unrealistic expectations:

- *Skills:* When a company purchases more-complex technologies, the contract usually includes professional consulting services so that the client can get up and running quickly to start seeing the benefits that were promised during the sales process. During this time, the company employees should be immersed in learning about the new technology and working very closely with the professional services consultants so that skills and knowledge are transferred and the company can sustain the technology after the consultant engagement ends. Even with simple software we subscribe to over the Internet, if it's not easy to use, the investments will be for naught.

  When it comes to service contracts, it's the responsibility of the vendor and client to ensure that the internal team has as much knowledge of the product as the consultant within a reasonable amount of time.

  A simple formula for success is to divide the project into thirds. One third of the time should be dedicated to ramp-up, another third allocated to self-sufficiency, and the final third should be dedicated to mastery.

  Let's assume that the average enterprise software project is scheduled to run for 18 months. You should expect that employees are close to being fully self-sufficient within 12 months. Not coincidentally, this time frame usually aligns with the software and service renewal license, so that's something to keep in mind as you negotiate the renewal.

- *Unrealistic expectations:* In an ideal world, the new technology easily blends with the existing technology a company has in place. When this isn't the case—which often happens—making everything work together can take a long time. This is often the point where companies begin to reassess their purchase as well as the skill set of the team responsible for integrating the technology. This is a critical juncture, because it can bring to light the shortcomings in the technology as well as the staff. And you know where fingers are likely to point if you're the software vendor.

To avoid losing the client, proving the value of the technology and creating demonstrable success that can be used to win other clients, it's important to establish milestones and report cards with the customer before any work starts.

It's easy and natural to want to just jump into the project. However, both sides need to agree on the road map as well as ongoing check-ins on progress. Otherwise, the project is vulnerable to failure in the form of a dissatisfied customer who may also have the right to pursue litigation.

With all these activities happening on a regular basis, you can see how the infrastructure continues to expand and contract. Even in instances where enterprise software has been displaced in favor of a competitor's offering, remnants probably will remain in the form of source code or customized applications. If that source code or those applications are not actively being used, make sure that they're no longer lingering and draining network resources.

Dispelling Seven Common IT Myths

Maintaining realistic expectations about technology is key to realizing productivity gains. With this in mind, following are seven common IT myths. The explanations clarify some of the more common misperceptions about what technology can and can't do:

■ *Computer science is an exact science.* The term "computer science" is a misnomer. I suggest we change the category name to the "art of computer science." If you think about software programming in terms of languages and how different aspects of those languages are linked to create an application, you start to see the real art behind computer science. Put another way, even though the English alphabet has only 26 letters, we manage to put those letters together in many different ways. Although we must follow processes and protocols in the art of computer science according to the programming language, we also have much freedom in how software is designed and developed. This is the stuff of innovation, yet it can also be a source of glitches. Perhaps if we infuse more business courses into the computer science curriculum to help put the efforts of software development in a business context, we can decrease some of the coding errors that arise.

■ *The next big software release will address the issues.* The software development process has four fixed dials: time, features, resources, and quality. Those dials are constantly fine-tuned as the software is developed, and any change to one dial affects the others.

For example, not properly estimating the time it takes to include certain features can affect the staff that's dedicated to the project, the quality of the final product, and the product release.

As is often the case, major product releases—those that end in a .0 or .5—tend to sacrifice quality to meet deadlines. This is why developers typically wait for the next point release from the vendor instead of using the major release version that is being marketed. This is a wise decision in many cases, but what can happen is the software vendor may release a series of point releases and patches to fix the known issues. IT departments must be careful to track the consistency in the version that's being used, because inconsistent versions that are being tweaked by a company's development team are ripe for the creation of glitches.

- *It works out of the box.* Retail software products are designed to work immediately as described, but enterprise software has varying degrees of customization. If you read any marketing material from an enterprise software vendor that touts its out-of-the box enterprise capabilities, think twice before you invest.

- *The code is documented.* This is a best practice to shoot for so that the company and any new team members will know exactly where the team left off in the development process. But it's unrealistic given the time constraints facing most IT staff. A lack of documentation contributes to knowledge drain across the board, but technology can be used to automate and track the more staid processes and mitigate some of these risks.

- *The documentation explains everything.* Documentation is critical to reducing the IT staff's learning curve, although there are varying degrees of quality when it comes to explaining how the software will work. This is why investing in professional consulting services and training classes to augment the team's existing skills and hands-on experience can be worthwhile.

- *All hackers are evil.* The definition of a hacker is a clever programmer.[9] Of course, the impact of some of that clever programming has created a negative connotation for the term. Once the trust hurdle has been cleared, however, there's something to be said for having someone on your team who knows the system's ins and outs, can find the holes and plug them, and will contribute to creating a stronger infrastructure.

- *The biggest threat is outside the walls.* We know about the threat of cyber attacks and cyber crime, and we are aware of the enemy within, but employees also can create cracks in the infrastructure.

In a 2010 survey of 305 CIOs conducted by Forrester Research, nearly 58 percent of security breaches were the result of an employee's losing a computing device or accidentally posting information on social networks.[10] Figure 4.2, from the Forrester report, breaks down employee security breaches by type.

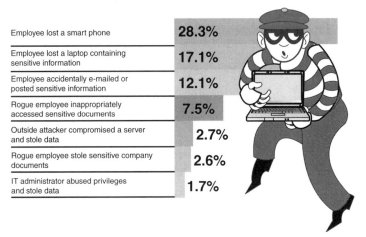

The Numerater

A Lost Cause

Information technology administrators rightly worry about outside threats to their networks and information, but they say the biggest threats come from inside, often the result of accidents or carelessness on the part of employees. A recent survey by Forrester Consulting, commissioned by Microsoft and RSA, backs up those fears. Forrester surveyed 305 high-level IT decision-makers worldwide, among other things asking them what types of security breaches they had experienced. Nearly 58 percent of the incidents were the result of an employee losing a computing device or accidentally posting sensitive information. Here is sample of the results.

Employee lost a smart phone	**28.3%**
Employee lost a laptop containing sensitive information	**17.1%**
Employee accidentally e-mailed or posted sensitive information	**12.1%**
Rogue employee inappropriately accessed sensitive documents	**7.5%**
Outside attacker compromised a server and stole data	**2.7%**
Rogue employee stole sensitive company documents	**2.6%**
IT administrator abused privileges and stole data	**1.7%**

Figure 4.2   *Types of employee security breaches*

Investing in the People and the Process

Technology will continue to flow into our businesses, and with that comes its inevitable flaws. Although the customers can't completely control how the software is developed, they can control how it is customized and managed once it's part of the IT infrastructure.

From an organizational point of view, this is best achieved through investments in the people and processes behind the technology. Following are suggestions for making the most of these IT investments.

A Company-Wide IT Council

Although the majority of the responsibility for technology rests with the IT department, it shouldn't end there. Many companies create cross-functional teams when they begin an extensive IT project, and these teams often are disbanded when the project goes live. They may regroup when something goes awry, but typically they don't meet on a regular basis. Other times, an entirely different team is assembled to evaluate a so-called new solution. These can be valuable in the short term, but they aren't entirely efficient or cost-effective if there are inconsistent views on how technology will be introduced and managed in a company.

A company-wide IT council would fairly represent each part of the organization on an ongoing basis and would continue to steer the direction of the technology that's in place to support the larger business goals.

Third-Party Auditing

Aside from what may be required by compliance regulations, more frequent audits on the IT infrastructure are worth considering. All too often we get caught up in our day-to-day activities and are too close to the technology to gain an unbiased view of what works, what could be improved, and where potential glitches may be lurking in the infrastructure. This audit would be conducted by external professional services consultants. They would be responsible for conducting customer feedback surveys and evaluating the IT infrastructure from a business and technical perspective.

IT Asset Inventory

An annual or biannual inventory of what exactly is in the infrastructure can help identify redundant technologies, ease the strain on the network for inactive applications and tools, and help efforts associated with documenting the code. Just be mindful that the inventory process is only to determine what is currently in place. It shouldn't disrupt the infrastructure until the cross-company IT council deems it appropriate.

Putting IT All Together

Having a deeper understanding of the complexities of the IT infrastructure will help companies derive more value from their technology investments.

Regardless of the current trends and hot acronyms that are being bandied about, the core aspects of building and sustaining a sound IT infrastructure are based on a solid foundation and the ability to enforce policies and procedures to strengthen that foundation.

With those guiding principles in place, a company can easily add more technology to the infrastructure without disrupting productivity or compromising customer satisfaction.

Endnotes

1. Capitalizing on Complexity. Insights from the 2010 IBM Global CEO Study. May 2010.
2. "The Digital Universe Decade." IDC Digital Universe Study sponsored by EMC. April 26, 2010.
3. Institute of Electronic Business E12 Conference. Lars Kirchhoff. December 1, 2008.
4. Interview with Steve Mills, IBM, by Jeff Papows. December 2009.
5. *Electronics*. "Cramming More Components onto Integrated Circuits." Gordon Moore. Volume 38, Number 8, April 19, 1965.
6. IBM. "Understanding 64-Bit PowerPC Architecture." http://www.ibm.com/developerworks/library/pa-microdesign/.

7. Intel® Itanium® 9300 Processor Raises Bar for Scalable, Resilient Mission-Critical Computing. http://www.intel.com/pressroom/archive/releases/2010/20100208comp.htm.

8. Interview with Elizabeth Grealy, Grealy Globalization Enterprises, by Kathleen Keating. May 2010.

9. *The New Hackers Dictionary*, 3rd Edition. Eric S. Raymond. MIT Press, 1996.

10. The Value of Corporate Secrets. How Compliance and Collaboration Affect Enterprise Perceptions of Risk. Forrester Research. March 2010.

CHAPTER 5

Technology's Influence: Past, Present, and Future

At this point, you may be thinking that technology has caused more harm than good. Granted, some of these glitches do read like a spy thriller or the makings of a cineplex blockbuster, but it's not all doom and gloom. After all, technology is the reason why we have electric power, clean water, public transportation, and so on.

There's no denying that the IT sector has been an engine for wealth creation and will continue to fuel the global economy for the foreseeable future. However, being able to maximize the rewards from this industry is not a given. It will require a closer look at where we are, where we've been, and what can potentially hold us back from where we want to go.

This chapter explores the following topics:

- Technology as an economic growth engine
- A brief history of the technology industry
- The impact of the Great Recession
- Critical success factors for the future

Technology as an Economic Growth Engine

Aside from some very public ups and downs, most notably the dotcom collapse, the information technology sector has consistently been a source of job creation and a contributor to the global economy. Looking at some facts and figures over the years, as well as future projections, we can expect this trend to continue.

A recent report from the U.S. Bureau of Labor Statistics found that employment of computer software engineers is projected to increase by 21 percent from 2008 to 2018, which is much faster than the average for all occupations and represents 295,000 new jobs.[1]

Along with increased job opportunities, IT-related salaries have steadily risen through the years. These numbers go beyond the standard cost-of-living increase or inflation. Consider that, in 1985, the software and related services sector in the United States employed 637,400 people, with an average annual salary of $30,031.[2] By 2007, that number had risen to 1.7 million people earning $85,600 annually, representing 195 percent of the national average.[3] Figure 5.1 illustrates total software and related services employment. Figure 5.2 shows the steady income growth of professionals in the U.S. software and services industry.[4]

In terms of the software industry's contributions to the gross domestic product, Figure 5.3, from the U.S. Bureau of Economic Analysis, shows a steady increase from the years 1995 to 2008.[5]

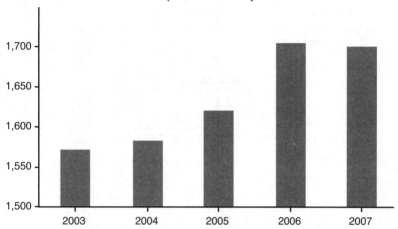

Figure 5.1   *Total U.S. software and related services employment*

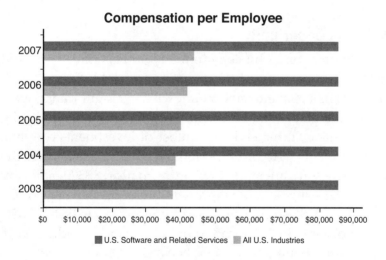

Figure 5.2   *Compensation per employee in the U.S. software industry*

	Line	1996	1998	2000	2002	2004	2006	2008
GDP	1	9433.9	10283.5	11226.0	11553.0	12263.8	12976.2	13312.2
GDP less final sales of software	2	9350.5	10134.1	11012.1	11341.1	12016.2	12694.6	12991.5
Final sales of software, total /1/	3	103.5	158.2	214.5	213.8	247.8	281.8	322.2
Personal consumption expenditures	4	2.2	5.2	7.6	9.4	12.7	17.1	20.6
Private fixed investment	5	78.5	122.8	172.4	173.4	204.6	227.1	257.0
Exports /2/	6	6.4	9.6	12.1	12.0	13.3	19.8	27.1
Less: Imports /2/	7	1.0	2.4	4.0	6.5	10.5	13.0	17.4
Government /3/	8	19.2	24.0	26.8	25.7	27.7	30.9	34.8
GDP	9	3.6	4.4	4.1	1.8	3.6	2.7	0.4
GDP less final sales of software	10	3.6	4.1	4.0	1.9	3.4	2.6	0.3
Difference	11	0.0	0.3	0.1	-0.1	0.2	0.1	0.1
Final sales of software, total /1/	12	17.2	19.7	12.8	-0.7	10.0	5.7	6.0
Final sales of software, total /1/	13	116.6	164.1	230.5	226.1	249.4	284.8	329.2
Personal consumption expenditures	14	6.5	8.5	11.0	11.8	13.5	16.1	17.7
Private fixed investment	15	85.5	126.0	184.5	183.0	205.7	229.8	264.1
Exports /2/	16	6.9	9.3	12.8	12.3	13.5	19.5	24.0
Less: Imports /2/	17	1.5	3.0	4.8	7.2	10.9	11.9	12.5
Government /3/	18	19.2	23.2	27.1	26.1	27.6	31.3	36.0

1. Software estimates include own-account production and exclude software embedded in equipment.
2. Includes software classified as goods and excludes software classified as services.
3. Excludes services of software, measured by consumption of fixed capital, for general government.

Figure 5.3 *GDP and final sales of software*

A Global Opportunity

The information technology industry will continue to benefit businesses and individuals around the world. Even though the 2008 financial industry meltdown had a significant impact across the globe, and IT spending experienced a dip during the recession, a tremendous number of investments continue to be made in IT. According to industry analysts at Gartner, the enterprise software market will grow to nearly $300 billion by 2013, averaging an annual growth rate of 5.4 percent.[6] Additionally, a 2009 study conducted by industry analysts at IDC and sponsored by Microsoft found that global spending on IT will create 5.8 million new jobs between 2009 and 2013.[7]

From the outside looking in, it appears that we don't lack for innovation or opportunity when it comes to the IT sector. However, several factors can interrupt progress and throw those future projections off course.

The Global Risks 2010 report from the World Economic Forum highlights the fact that underinvesting in infrastructure is one of the biggest risks to the global economy.[8] From a broader perspective, infrastructure in this context refers not only to technology but also to other sectors that sustain us, including energy and agriculture. The report also outlines the impact of the growing interconnectedness among all areas of risk, including economics, geopolitics, environment, society, and technology. That interconnectedness, when combined with the financial meltdown, increases the need for greater global governance across governments and the private sector. However, gaps in this governance exist.

When applied appropriately, technology can help sustain the interconnectedness and enable governments and businesses to work together more closely to close governance gaps.

The Past Is Prologue: A Brief History of the IT Industry

To better prepare for the future, we must first understand the past. With this in mind, let's take a moment to recap three of the most critical evolutionary phases in the IT industry:

- The mighty mainframe and the back office
- Revolution in the front office
- Massive globalization through the Internet era

The Mighty Mainframe and the Back Office

The back-office era gained momentum in the 1960s as companies with large budgets invested upwards of $1 million to get their hands on a mainframe. These mainframes were housed in large air-conditioned rooms and were tended to by teams of technicians wearing white coats. These technicians were responsible for performing what was then considered sophisticated data analysis using punch cards.

As an aside, history buffs will be quick to point out Herman Hollerith and the role of punch cards in the 1890 census.[9] Hollerith founded the Computer Tabulating Recording Company, which later was renamed International Business Machines Corporation (IBM).[10]

From the day-to-day view of computing in the office, the mainframe was just beginning to change the shape of things in the 1960s. The industry responded to the high costs of the mainframe with the introduction of minicomputers, which were smaller and less powerful yet still a viable alternative. The first minicomputer, created by Digital Equipment Corporation, debuted in 1965[11] and was priced at approximately $16,000. Although the minicomputer and its cousin, the mid-range, are rarely seen today, their accessibility and power helped expand the role of computers in business.

The mid-1960s and 1970s were primarily characterized by the then-radical deployment of mainframe and minicomputers to automate and organize a wide range of back-office functions such as accounting, inventory tracking, payroll, and compiling human resources data. By today's standards, these were simple tasks. As decision makers at companies became more aware of the computer's ability to help streamline back-office functions, technology in the workplace started to take on a larger role.

Today, the power of the mainframe has yet to be usurped. The mainframe has been in place at some companies for decades due to its strength, which is sustained by the leading mainframe providers. These include IBM; Hewlett-Packard through its acquisition of Compaq, which acquired Digital Equipment Corporation; and Oracle through its acquisition of Sun Microsystems.

Given the life span of the mainframe, it's almost impossible to grasp just how much information it has been able to help companies accumulate and process over the years. The mainframe represents a significant portion of a company's IT budget, and it's becoming even more expensive to maintain. These costs include the following:

- Staffing
- MIPS consumption
- Rising energy costs

Staffing

As we've discussed, a potentially costly expense is associated with the IT knowledge drain, especially when it comes to COBOL programmers who are essential to the ongoing maintenance of mainframes. While the mainframe will continue to be a mainstay, the shortage of skilled programmers and those who are interested in supporting them will affect nearly every business that even remotely relies on these technology workhorses.

MIPS Consumption

MIPS stands for millions of instructions per second and is generally used to refer to the processing speed and performance of larger computers. In this context, we're referring to how quickly and efficiently a mainframe can process a transaction. From an economical point of view, MIPS helps you determine how much money each of those transactions will cost to process. The more data we have, the more data we need to process, which drives up MIPS consumption. Reducing the cost of MIPS is a priority for companies, especially as we continue to increase our data transaction loads on the mainframe.

Rising Energy Costs

The size of the mainframe and its extreme processing power require a significant amount of energy to run, which drives up the cost of ownership. In many instances, mainframes are located offsite in a data center. So not only do you pay for the offsite location, but data center energy costs can be 100 times higher than those for typical buildings.[12] Companies are very mindful of the rising costs of energy and how that affects the environment, especially since data centers will account for 3 percent of total U.S. electricity consumption in 2011.[13] Businesses and government agencies are addressing this issue, yet it will remain a concern for the foreseeable future.

Revolution in the Front Office

As the role of technology became more widespread, partly as a result of the productivity gains achieved through the mainframe, we entered the era of the front office. This expansion was primarily the result of the mass adoption of personal computers in the 1980s.

Much like the mainframe automated back-end tasks, the personal computer put similar processing power on the desktops of knowledge workers and streamlined the bulk of clerical tasks. Traditional office tools such as typewriters, accounting ledgers, and overhead projectors were replaced by word processing software, spreadsheets, and presentation applications.

This second wave of IT innovation formed the foundation of today's integrated enterprises. Although the desktop experiences of individual knowledge workers were clearly enhanced during this era, it wasn't until the introduction of e-mail and voice mail in the 1990s that technology really became front and center in the workplace. Thankfully—and, on some days, regrettably—these advances paved the way for the always-on businesses of today.

Massive Globalization Through the Internet Era

The third wave is most clearly defined by the Internet gold rush. As we saw with previous technology-inspired booms such as railroads in the 1840s, automobiles and radio in the 1920s, and transistor electronics in the 1950s, the Internet era led to new wealth-creation models.

Just how much wealth creation are we talking about? Looking at U.S. Census Bureau data, the information/communications/technology-producing industries contributed $855 billion to the $11.6 trillion total GDP in 2008. This number in 1990 was a mere $100.6 billion of the $7.1 trillion total GDP.[14]

Equally important, if not more so, were the new business models that the Internet introduced as easier access to the global economy represented significant opportunities. The competition that sprang up from seemingly unexpected places helped fuel innovation and a focus on customer service. Not only are we now faced with competition from all over the globe, but we also have to contend with dissatisfied customers alerting the world to their experiences.

Changing Business Models

Amazon.com's emergence during this period is worth a closer look, because the company was transparent about the fact that it wouldn't become profitable for several years. In a climate of instant gratification and get-rich-quick ideas, Amazon.com proved the importance of a sound business plan. Meanwhile, a good many dotcoms imploded around Amazon, and bricks-and-mortar establishments scrambled to figure out their online strategy. After an eight-year stretch, not only did Amazon prove its naysayers wrong, but it also now dominates the e-commerce market.

Just look at how Amazon has grown through the years in book sales alone. Figure 5.4 compares Amazon with leading booksellers Barnes & Noble and Borders.[15] Amazon is one of many companies that emerged successfully from the Internet era. It proves that you should never underestimate the power of a well-formed strategy—and, more importantly, you should never take your position for granted.

Conversely, as the world got more flat vis-à-vis the Internet, casualties occurred in existing business models. For example, to serve an overseas customer base, Lotus was burning, assembling, shrink-wrapping, and shipping software CDs. The job creation associated with managing and packaging the warehouse inventory contributed to the Commonwealth of Massachusetts' economy as well as the economies of overseas distributors. As the Internet evolved, shrink-wrapped software was replaced by simple downloads, eliminating the need for warehouses. This directly affected the livelihood of employees in adjacent industries, including printing, design, packaging, and manufacturing.

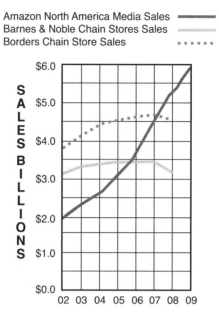

Figure 5.4   *Amazon's sales growth versus major competitors*

In the latter half of the 2000s, we saw another shift brought on by Web 2.0. The explosion of social media tools, for better or worse, dramatically changed how we create, interpret, digest, and share information and news throughout companies and with our friends and family.

When our traditional media outlets shrank or disappeared, we saw the creation of smaller, niche communities of experts. As the traditional media playing field was leveled, up popped thousands of smaller outlets that filled the gap with up-to-the-minute news, information, and speculation. Instead of reading one national newspaper, we now customize our news feeds based on certain bloggers, discussion forums, Twitterati, and highly focused media outlets.

Along with the benefits of those customized feeds comes the deluge of data that needs to be analyzed, categorized, and otherwise waded through for it to make sense. The challenge for all of us is keeping up with this volume. Consumers must manage information and properly categorize it as it relates to their jobs and interests. Also, since the second era in computing boosted productivity through personal computers, knowledge workers are now constantly creating new and different forms of data to perform their jobs. From an IT perspective, the exponential growth in data is draining the network and adding to the mainframe's workload. Given all the information that needs to be managed, I suspect many IT departments often feel like some days at work are like a never-ending game of whack-a-mole.

With every major shift in the IT industry, compromises had a domino effect on parts of, if not entire, tangential industries. Some are more obvious, such as the situation with Lotus packaging or the economics of the traditional publishing model, which also affects advertising agencies, printers, and even college journalism curricula.

Other shifts are less public and more widespread and slowly creep up on us—at least, that's how the Great Recession initially appeared.

The Impact of the Great Recession

In late 2008 and throughout 2009, the phrase "too big to fail" made its way from financial regulation circles to dinner tables as bad news continued to be reported about the collapse of the financial industry as we knew it. Along with the news came a crash course in economics. We soon learned about the subprime lending that led to the near-collapse of the housing market, as well as what overleveraging and opaque financial reports mean to the sustainability of an economy. We also learned that the recession actually began in 2007.[16]

Those who were less interested in complex economic models simply wanted to know why the cost of commodities such as oil and food was going through the roof while uncertainties about employment and retirement funds were looming. When simple explanations were not so simple, lots of fingers were pointed toward individuals and groups who were deemed responsible for what is now viewed as the deepest and widest recession since the Great Depression.

Looking to identify one source or a single inciting incident for the recession is impossible, because various factors came together to create the situation. Some blame goes as far back as the Carter and Clinton Administrations. Others believe it was the result of the housing boom and the subprime lending that was made available to unqualified consumers who eventually defaulted on their charge cards and mortgages.

There's no doubt that the recession of the late 2000s will continue to be studied in classrooms and boardrooms for years to come. In light of the many dimensions that led to the recession and sectors that were affected by it, the following sections take a closer look at it from an IT perspective by exploring these topics:

- Bernie Madoff: a catalyst for change
- Massive mergers and acquisitions pressure the IT infrastructure
- The benefits of transparency in business processes

Bernie Madoff: A Catalyst for Change

Greater transparency may have stemmed or perhaps halted the extent of the damage caused by Bernie Madoff, a former Wall Street investment advisor and arguably the most widely hated white-collar criminal.

Madoff was a stockbroker and chairman of the NASDAQ stock market before he ran the world's largest hedge fund. The hedge fund turned out to be the longest and most widespread Ponzi scheme in history[17] as Madoff bilked clients out of more than $65 billion under the guise of financial investments and advice. Many signs of misconduct and complaints were brought before the public.[18] The U.S. Securities and Exchange Commission (SEC)[19] admitted that Madoff's financial activities were illegal. Unfortunately, the scam wasn't properly addressed until it was too late.

From an IT perspective, we learned that one of Madoff's tricks was to punch fake trades into an old midrange computer. Madoff controlled all access to the computer and entered share prices that aligned with his so-called financial returns.[20] Because he rigged the computer, the trades and reports looked accurate to the untrained eye. The fact that Madoff was also viewed as a Wall Street trading technology pioneer helped him carry on his behavior for decades.

Madoff's behavior begs the questions that many of us are still asking. Where was the transparency into Madoff's dealings, and where was the transparency within the IT infrastructure? The SEC has instituted new policies and procedures since Madoff was discovered to be a fraud. With its Post-Madoff Reforms,[21] the Commission has revamped nearly every aspect of its operations in an effort to provide greater transparency and to mitigate the risks that allowed Madoff to carry out his activities.

From an IT point of view, the SEC reforms call for more centralized management of information and tighter controls to more effectively alert officials to potential red flags. The SEC's actions, in my view, underscore the importance of IT governance to help increase visibility into computer-related transactions.

Is another Madoff situation lurking in an IT infrastructure? We may not know until it's too late. As a body that oversees the health of the financial industry, the SEC is in a position to effect more change from an IT perspective. Therefore, backroom computers like the one that Madoff used are no longer viable unless they meet specific IT governance requirements mandated by the Federal government. If IT governance principles were applied to and enforced in the infrastructures that are responsible for executing financial transactions, there would be a greater likelihood that those red flags would be identified before the transactions were executed or consumer complaints were formally reported to the SEC.

Massive Mergers and Acquisitions Pressure the IT Infrastructure

One of the sectors most dramatically affected by the recession was financial services. According to Thomas Philippon, an economist at New York University's Stern School of Business, the financial sector lost 548,000 jobs, or 6.6 percent of that industry's workforce, during the Great Recession.[22]

With the sector's consolidation came significant mergers that required massive IT integration to bring together the newly formed companies. Some of the bigger ones included Bank of America's $50 billion merger with Merrill Lynch[23] and Wells Fargo's $15.1 billion merger with Wachovia.[24]

The term massive undertaking is an understatement when it comes to accurately portraying the work associated with merging the back-end systems of financial institutions without disrupting service to customers.

As any IT professional can attest, bringing together two different organizations of any size is never as straightforward as it may initially appear, even when the most comprehensive strategy has been mapped out by IT and business professionals. This is especially true when you consider that you're often bringing together two completely different infrastructures, cultures, and sets of business processes.

Although overlaps may occur in the technology that's in place at the individual companies, there will be variables in terms of how the software was customized to address specific business functions that are part of the fabric of those individual organizations.

Still, a merger also presents opportunities, because it forces you to evaluate best practices, policies, and existing technologies. What is often uncovered are what I call "potholes" in the infrastructure. These are the small, often contained glitches that may be found in applications, in web services, or within parts of a platform. They often go undetected because the information gets to its intended recipients—eventually. Only when these potholes disrupt the flow of data or stall productivity do we address them.

At the heart of any successful integration project is the software code. After all, the applications and systems can't work together properly if the code is faulty. In many instances, the code may not be completely erroneous, but it does go against internal IT policies and best practices and, sometimes, better judgment.

Even if the code does pass inspection, it will eventually show signs of shoddy workmanship in the form of system failures, software glitches, and the like. Since integration can be an extensive and expensive project, and parts of it tend to be tedious, you can automate some of the more mundane tasks. Yet you have to determine how much you want to automate and how much will still require real live project team leaders to oversee the process. The goal is to strike the right balance between the two.

As companies continue to merge and more devices and computers are connected to the Internet, we will see more of these "potholes," because they are no longer isolated. However, if we know where they are, we can do something about them before it's too late.

Mergers and the Disappearing Bank Balance

One of these oversights in the IT infrastructure affected customers of TDBank in 2009 when it was in the midst of its integration with Commerce Bank.[25] Thousands of banking customers were locked out of their accounts and couldn't accurately reconcile their statements. This happened because of a glitch that didn't accurately track balances and caused delays in recognizing automatic payroll deposit checks.

Martin Focazio and his wife were customers of both TDBank and Commerce Bank at the time of the post-merger integration. He shared their experiences with me for this book.[26] Martin had set up his payroll direct deposit to go into his TDBank account, and it had successfully worked this way for years. Since the Focazios are diligent about checking their bank balance every day, his wife noticed immediately when the bank didn't record the direct deposit.

After Focazio's wife made several phone calls to TDBank and was put on hold for up to 40 minutes, Martin turned to Twitter to find out if anybody else had been affected by this glitch. He discovered that other customers had the same experience, though he had yet to be notified by the bank. While he scrambled to withdraw cash from other sources to cover monthly expenses, it was not the most convenient situation, to say the least.

"We were lucky that we had the funds to cover our bills," said Focazio. "A lot of people these days don't, and while the bank said they'd cover interest and fees, that's not a lot of help to people who will be charged high interest on their late balances and can potentially put their credit scores at risk. It's a downward spiral if you're living paycheck to paycheck and are hit with a series of late fees and high interest rates because the bank made a mistake."

By consistently calling the bank and checking their balance online, the Focazios realized that the issue was later fixed, yet they never received notification from the bank beyond a posting on its website. Then, according to Focazio, "the exact same thing happened two weeks later." This second offense is what led the Focazios to switch banks. I suspect that they were not the only customers to do this.

These issues go beyond the financial services industry. Dana Gardner, IT analyst and founder of Interarbor Solutions, shared his opinion on this topic and on the impact of glitches during our interview.[27] "Increasingly, when I personally find fault with a business, process, government, service, or product, I think about how well the company, community, government, or ecosystem develops software.

"If I'm on hold for 20 minutes when I call a global bank for a reason that legitimately requires a customer service representative, that's a software life cycle failure," said Gardner.

"When I buy a flat-panel TV and it takes me four hours to make it work with the components, that's a software life cycle failure. When I wait for three hours for what was supposed to be a one-hour brake pad replacement, that's a software life cycle failure. The degree to which software and processes are mutually supportive and governed determines how things fall apart, or how they need to be fixed."

Now is the time for an increased focus on preventive best practices in IT across all industries—before the recent trends in highly visible computer glitches described here become truly debilitating.

The Benefits of Transparency in Business Processes

The situation with Madoff, as well as the need to avoid glitches in everyday business transactions, point out the growing need for transparency in the IT infrastructure. The complementary combination of IT governance and compliance can help deliver that transparency. Yet where it's applied and how much is required depend on the industry and the company itself.

A common misperception is that introducing a greater level of transparency into the infrastructure requires that a company hire a team of experts and spend unnecessary money on adding more technology to an already complex IT environment. When applied properly, compliance and IT governance can enable a company to more effectively mitigate any risks to the business before they impede performance or erode the bottom line.

This argument becomes stronger when you realize that nearly 55 percent of a company's software applications budget is consumed by supporting ongoing operations.[28] If some of the maintenance efforts can be executed using automated governance, this can free up the IT staff to focus on more strategic efforts.

Additionally, with greater transparency into the IT infrastructure, we will be better able to determine the source of the glitch for greater accountability. We may also be able to retire the convenient and sometimes questionable "It must have been a computer glitch" excuse.

When we step back and take a closer look at the changes in business driven by technology in just over a few decades, we're reminded of how complex our infrastructures can be. If the introduction and on-going maintenance of technology is not managed properly, we are leaving our businesses and customers more vulnerable to the creation and distribution of glitches.

Although we can't go back in time, we can move forward by creating greater transparency into the IT infrastructure. This transparency must be delivered across the entire company and not trapped in a department or division. Otherwise, we risk perpetuating the cycle of silo-based information that inhibits growth and productivity and ultimately leads to failed IT projects.

According to Michael Krigsman, CEO of Asuret, a consultancy specialized in improving the success rate of enterprise technology initiatives, "Most IT projects fail before they even begin. Poor governance, lack of clear project strategy and goals, insufficient executive support, and so on militate against project success."[31]

Critical Success Factors for the Future

In the interest of illustrating the hidden impact of faulty software, we've highlighted technology's influence on the global economy, covered the history of the industry, and touched on the latest recession. Here are the critical takeaways from these inflection points in the IT industry:

- One of the keys to sustaining global growth is to have the IT sector lend its expertise to ensure continued connectedness among governments and businesses worldwide. The IT industry should consider donating services and technology to support connectedness among the areas most in need of closing governance gaps.

- Energy efficiency will remain a top priority for businesses. It's worth considering working only with vendors that can demonstrate their ability to support the most energy-efficient IT infrastructures. In the U.S., the Environmental Protection Agency and the Department of Energy have created Energy Star label certifications for the data center, which will help clients validate the efficiency of their IT provider.[29]

■ The financial services sector, while already heavily regulated, could benefit from additional IT governance. This includes the federal enforcement of technology-driven policies that instantly alert the proper government agencies and overseeing boards to stop potentially fraudulent activity.

■ Mergers and acquisitions will continue to impact the IT infrastructure. But companies shouldn't wait for a merger or other external force to assess the health of their infrastructure. Build transparency into the IT infrastructure so that you always have an up-to-the-minute status on all activities.

■ Successful mergers and acquisitions are possible when a cross-functional team is dedicated to the integration strategy. This includes a focus on the customer experience and a well-paced transition that occurs in time to allow the integration to be tested in various user scenarios before the system goes live.

Technology will continue to influence global markets, but we're still in the nascent stages of our globally connected economy. Some 60 percent of the world's population has never had contact with information technologies, and the majority of content that is being disseminated over the Internet is meant for developed societies.[30]

This data will change as the industry continues to evolve. However, the benefits will be negated unless IT organizations and government leaders make a concerted effort to eliminate the obvious obstacles to advancement. These obstacles include lack of governance, the need for more organized task forces dedicated to global IT advancement, and greater transparency across all business processes.

Endnotes

1. United States Bureau of Labor Statistics. Occupational Outlook Handbook 2010–11.

2. United States Business Software Alliance.

3. Organization for Economic and Co-Operation and Development. STAN Database for STructural ANalysis (STAN) Indicators Database, ed. 2008.

4. Ibid.

5. U.S. Bureau of Economic Analysis. GDP Software Investment and Prices. August 27, 2009.

6. Gartner. Forecast: Enterprise Software Markets, Worldwide, 2008–2013, 1Q09 Update. March 16, 2009.

7 IDC. "Aid to Recovery: The Economic Impact of IT, Software, and the Microsoft Ecosystem on the Economy." October 2009.

8. World Economic Forum. "Global Risks 2010." January 2010.

9. U.S. Library of Congress. Hollerith's Electric Tabulating and Sorting Machine. 1895.

10. U.S. Census Bureau: History. Herman Hollerith. http://www.census.gov/history/www/census_then_now/notable_alumni/herman_hollerith.html.

11. Digital Computing Timeline. http://vt100.net/timeline/1965.html.

12. Lawrence Berkeley National Laboratory. Data Center Energy Management. http://hightech.lbl.gov/DCTraining/.

13. U.S. Environmental Protection Agency. Report to Congress on Server and Data Center Energy Efficiency. August 2, 2007. http://hightech.lbl.gov/documents/DATA_CENTERS/epa-datacenters.pdf.

14. U.S. Census Bureau. Gross Domestic Product by Industry Accounts, Real Value Added by Industry. Release date April 28, 2009.

15. Amazon growth chart. http://www.fonerbooks.com/booksale.htm.

16. National Bureau of Economic Research. Determination of the December 2007 Peak in Economic Activity. http://www.nber.org/cycles/dec2008.html.

17. *New York Times*. "Madoff Is Sentenced to 150 Years for Ponzi Scheme." Diana B. Henriques. June 29, 2009.

18. Barron's. "Don't Ask, Don't Tell." Erin Arvedlund. May 7, 2001. http://online.barrons.com/article/SB989019667829349012.html.

19. "The World's Largest Hedge Fund Is a Fraud." November 7, 2005 submission to the SEC. Madoff Securities, LLC. United States Securities and

Exchange Commission. http://www.sec.gov/news/studies/2009/oig-509/exhibit-0293.pdf.

20. *Too Good to Be True: The Rise and Fall of Bernie Madoff.* Erin Arvedlund. Portfolio Hardcover, 2009.

21. United States Securities and Exchange Commission Post-Madoff Reforms. http://www.sec.gov/spotlight/secpostmadoffreforms.htm.

22. *Wall Street Journal.* "Even if the Economy Improves, Many Jobs Won't Come Back." Justin Lahart. January 12, 2010.

23. Bank of America press release. Bank of America Buys Merrill Lynch Creating Unique Financial Services Firm. http://newsroom.bankofamerica.com/index.php?s=43&item=8255.

24. Wells Fargo press release. Wells Fargo, Wachovia Agree to Merge. https://www.wellsfargo.com/press/2008/20081003_Wachovia.

25. Network World. "TDBank Struggles to Fix Computer Glitch." Jaikumar Vijayan. October 2, 2009. http://www.networkworld.com/news/2009/100209-td-bank-struggles-to-fix.html.

26. Interview with Martin Focazio by Kathleen Keating. January 2010.

27. Interview with Dana Gardner by Kathleen Keating. January 2010.

28. Forrester Research. "The State of Enterprise Software and Emerging Trends: 2010." February 12, 2010.

29. U.S. Environmental Protection Agency, U.S. Department of Energy. Enterprise Server and Data Center Energy Efficiency Initiatives. http://www.energystar.gov/index.cfm?c=prod_development.server_efficiency.

30. World Economic Forum. Update: 2008. http://www.weforum.org/en/knowledge/Industries/InformationTechnologies/KN_SESS_SUMM_23553?url=/en/knowledge/Industries/InformationTechnologies/KN_SESS_SUMM_23553.

31. Interview with Michael Krigsman by Kathleen Keating. May 2010.

CHAPTER 6

The Mobility and Network Maze

"Great discoveries and improvements invariably involve the cooperation of many minds. I may be given credit for having blazed the trail, but when I look at the subsequent developments I feel the credit is due to others rather than to myself."

—Alexander Graham Bell

While disruptive technologies, monopolies, investors, and first-mover advantage were the talk of the '90s, they also were quite the center of attention in the '70s—the 1870s.

After all, the invention of the telephone led to some of the biggest technology disruptions of the 20th century. Alexander Graham Bell was one of many inventors who believed that the telegraph's ability to send and receive messages through code could be expanded to include transmitting voice.

Bell was naturally inquisitive and partially inspired by his future father-in-law's financial incentive to disrupt Western Union's telegraph monopoly. His invention of the telephone set in motion the rudimentary beginnings of today's voice and data communications.

Fast-forward to today. The telephone has migrated from a static tool to a mobile device that's like an appendage for many of us. Yet the infrastructure to support the mobile explosion faces serious challenges. This chapter explores the following topics:

- The increasing dependence on mobile technologies

- The impact of mobile access on the evolving IT infrastructure

- Sustaining an infrastructure to support current and future technologies

The Increasing Dependence on Mobile Technologies

Advances in mobile devices are driving up the dependence on mobile technologies despite the fragility of cell phones and wireless connectivity. The infrastructures to support them will be further strained in the near future as a result of the growth of the mobile Internet and the rise of teleworkers.

The Growth of the Mobile Internet

There's no denying the increase in connectedness to corporate infrastructures and the Internet using smartphones, tablet computers, laptops, and other mobile devices. Just one small slice of this market, smartphones, is growing at a rapid pace. Table 6.1 illustrates just how quickly the smartphone market grew from 2008 to 2009.[1]

Table 6.1   *Worldwide Mobile Phone Sales, 2008 and 2009*

Company	2009 Sales	2009 Market Share	2008 Sales	2008 Market Share
Nokia	440,881.6	36.4%	472,314.9	38.6%
Samsung	235,772.0	19.5%	199,324.3	16.3%
LG	122,055.3	10.1%	102,789.1	8.4%
Motorola	58,475.2	4.8%	106,522.4	8.7%
Sony Ericsson	54,873.4	4.5%	93,106.1	7.6%
Others	299,179.2	24.7%	248,196.1	20.3%
Total	1,211,236.6	100.0%	1,222,252.9	100.0 %

The prospects for continued prosperity in the smartphone market are strong and indicate that smartphones are increasingly being used to download and share information. This makes sense, considering that the growth in the mobile device market has been exponentially faster than any previous computing technology.[2] Not to mention the highly successful launch of Apple's iPad in 2010, which also relies on the infrastructure to access information, videos, music, and games.

Speaking of the infrastructure strain, as you may recall, the iPad launch was followed by concerns about AT&T's ability to handle the additional network demands the new product would create. Five days after the iPad launch, Phil Bellaria and John Leibovitz of the Federal Communications Commission (FCC) posted the following on their blog:

"With the iPad pointing to even greater demand for mobile broadband on the horizon, we must ensure that network congestion doesn't choke off a service that consumers clearly find so appealing, or frustrate mobile broadband's ability to keep us competitive in the global broadband economy."[3]

What all of this adds up to is a rapidly growing mobile Internet that will be bigger than the desktop Internet by 2015. Figure 6.1 illustrates how the mobile Internet is outpacing desktop Internet adoption.[4] But can the networks keep up with the demand? If not, what are the consequences of failure?

Frustrated Carriers, Frustrated Consumers

With the rising adoption rates of mobile devices comes a decline in the quality of service and performance offered by the carriers. A 2010 consumer satisfaction survey conducted by J.D. Power and Associates found that the biggest issues with quality of service involve dropped calls, interference, failed connections, voice distortion, echoes, and lack of immediate notification of voicemail and text messages.[5]

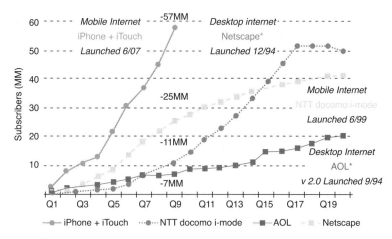

Figure 6.1 *Morgan Stanley: mobile Internet outpaces desktop Internet adoption*

As consumers rely more on their mobile devices to download data as opposed to using them for person-to-person calls, the issues of access, bandwidth, and network reliability come to the forefront.

In December 2009, AT&T President and Chief Executive Officer, Mobility and Consumer Markets Ralph de la Vega spoke about the issue of bandwidth availability at the UBS 37th Annual Global Media and Communications Conference. de la Vega told financial analysts that the "amount of growth and data that we are seeing in wireless data is unprecedented."[6]

de la Vega explained that AT&T is considering various options to address its service issues. Although he didn't provide full details, public reports mention that efforts are under way to add 2,000 cell sites,[7] and there is the potential for a tiered pricing structure. Additionally, AT&T is aiming to further educate consumers about their data consumption through the "Mark the Spot" iPhone application, which lets users report problems such as dropped calls and spotty coverage.

In his speech, however, de la Vega also stated that three percent of AT&T smartphone customers represent 40 percent of the network's data traffic.[8] In outlining how AT&T can more effectively handle the traffic, he said, "We're going to try to focus on making sure we give incentives to those small percentages to either reduce or modify their usage so they don't crowd out the customers on those same cell sites."

Many consumers interpreted AT&T's efforts to educate customers about data consumption as a request to decrease data downloads. Shortly after AT&T addressed the UBS audience, technology industry journalist Dan Lyons introduced "Operation Chokehold" through his satirical blog, The Secret Diary of Steve Jobs.[9] Initially meant to be a joke, following is the text from the blog post:

Subject: Operation Chokehold

On Friday, December 18, at noon Pacific time, we will attempt to overwhelm the AT&T data network and bring it to its knees. The goal is to have every iPhone user (or as many as we can) turn on a data intensive app and run that app for one solid hour. Send the message to AT&T that we are sick of their substandard network and sick of their abusive comments. The idea is we'll create a digital flash mob. We're calling it Operation Chokehold. Join us and speak truth to power!

It wasn't long before Operation Chokehold had more than 4,000 Facebook fans and the FCC got involved. Jamie Barnett, the FCC's Chief of Public Safety and Homeland Security, read the following statement to ABC News:

FCC Statement in Response to Operation Chokehold

"Threats of this nature are serious, and we caution the public to use common sense and good judgment when accessing the Internet from their commercial mobile devices. To purposely try to disrupt or negatively impact a network with ill intent is irresponsible and presents a significant public safety concern."[10]

Although Lyons wrote some additional blog posts regarding less extreme alternatives to Operation Chokehold, this was one message that made its way through the network. In this instance, both the consumers and the service provider have a point. As customers rely more and more on their mobile devices, they expect unlimited data access, as outlined in their contracts. Meanwhile, the service providers are doing their best to respond to consumer demand, yet they can be hindered by their own infrastructures.

The Rise of Teleworkers

With collaboration software and mobile devices everywhere, as well as increased awareness of our carbon footprint, it's easy to understand the rise in the number of teleworkers. Figure 6.2 shows this steady increase from 2002 to 2008.[11]

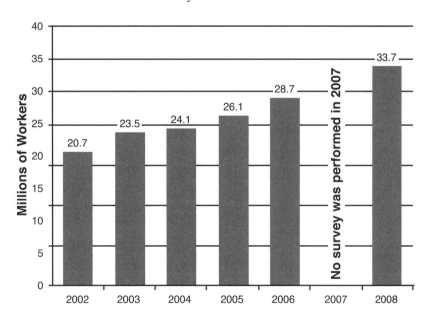

Figure 6.2   *U.S. teleworkers: WorldatWork Telework Trendlines 2009 survey brief, February 2009*

The network traffic from teleworkers isn't completely about the number of employees trying to remotely log on to the company intranet or check their e-mail. It's more about their role as knowledge workers and how much data they are downloading, creating, and sending to colleagues. If you've ever patiently waited for a large presentation or audio file to open on your desktop, you know how critical bandwidth and speed are to productivity.

Since we can expect that the number of telecommuters will continue to increase, we need to be sure that our infrastructures really can accommodate this growing population in the workforce. For many employers, this isn't just about accommodating the ability to work from home on an intermittent basis. This is about the war for talent and making sure you can effectively recruit and retain the best employees for your team, regardless of where they choose to live.

Supporting the Road Warriors

Legions of employees such as insurance investigators, ambulance drivers, and sales reps typically don't work in a traditional office but depend on the speed and resiliency of the network, quality of data, and available bandwidth capacity for their livelihood. Following are two examples that illustrate the importance of a sound infrastructure to support employees on the road. The first example is from the commercial trucking industry, and the second is from the New York City police department.

Data Quality in Commercial Trucking

Perhaps you've seen a truck stuck under a bridge or an 18-wheeler trying to back up on a busy stretch of road. These types of maneuvers often lead to accidents because the drivers are unfamiliar with the area or have inaccurate information about the route. Even though professional truck drivers possess a truck-specific global positioning system (GPS) and a mobile device, they need to be assured that the software that generates the routes doesn't contain a glitch and that they can instantly connect to the office network in the event of an emergency.

For example, when the I-35W Mississippi River bridge collapsed on August 1, 2007, it affected river, road, bicycle, and pedestrian passageways as well as air transit.[12] Professional truckers who were customers of Maptuit, a supplier of real-time commercial navigation software, were rerouted within minutes. Had the update to the truckers on that route been stalled due to a network capacity issue or faulty data, the trucks could have potentially blocked ambulances from entry to the site, thereby compounding the already tragic scene in Minneapolis. Not to mention the impact on the goods in transport and their company's bottom line.

According to Rick Turek, chief technology officer at Maptuit, it's the responsibility of management to explain to software developers the ramifications of a glitch if the code they're working on will eventually play a role in the business and personal lives of others. Turek explains, "When it comes to our software development processes, every member of the team understands that a mistake can impact the physical well-being of the driver. It can also potentially cost a trucking fleet millions of dollars."

Technology shortcomings, whether they are due to flawed software or simply the limitations of the devices themselves, should not be discovered as hazardous materials or other precious cargo is en route.

Sorry, Wrong House Raid

The other example of how a computer glitch can have an impact on the safety of citizens happened to 83-year-old Walter Martin and his 82-year-old wife, Rose. The law-abiding Brooklyn, New York couple were the victims of a computer glitch that started when the police department tried to automate its computer system that tracks crime complaints and internal police information.[13]

The glitch that got into the New York City police department's database in 2002 resulted in 50 raids on the Martins' home over a period of eight years. When the police input the names of suspects into its database, the glitch directed them to the Martins' home. The definitive source of the glitch was never confirmed, yet it's likely that a criminal suspect either lived in the home at one point or provided it as a false address.

The Martins have since been assured that the glitch has been fixed. But these types of missteps can distract our police and other public servants from protecting citizens who actually need help.

The situation with the Martins is not a straightforward mobile glitch. However, when you think about the validity of the data that law enforcement officers rely upon as they perform their jobs outside of traditional office walls, you realize how a seemingly simple glitch can have a strong ripple effect.

The Impact of Mobile Access on the Evolving IT Infrastructure

Just as we are seeing a surge in our connectedness as individuals, we're also seeing a rise in businesses' reliance on remote access to the IT infrastructure. As much as we can recognize the productivity benefits of this fact, we are also further straining our infrastructures due to limited bandwidth. Let's take a closer look at these influences, which include the following:

- Cloud computing
- The mobile cloud
- The full spectrum

Cloud Computing

More and more companies that were previously limited by technical and financial resources are taking advantage of subscription-based software offerings, also known as software as a service (SaaS). Supported by the cloud computing platform, SaaS is a way to host applications and services on a shared, sometimes remote server, and access them through a "cloud." Those applications and services ideally can be accessed from nearly any computer anywhere in the world.

If you've been around technology for a while, you know that the concept of cloud computing is not new. Businesses have consistently relied on shared resources—specifically, networks—to house information in the interest of saving money.

Yet cloud computing makes access to applications and services easier and cheaper and further reduces the costs of managing those applications internally. This is ideal for applications that are used by many employees and that don't require intensive programming to make them work. Some of these applications include word processing and spreadsheets, as well as sales-related tools and customer relationship management packages.

At first it appeared that cloud computing was ideal for small businesses that wanted to alleviate the work associated with application management and the associated high administration costs and licensing fees. However, large organizations also see significant cost savings and efficiency benefits in making part of their infrastructure available through a cloud.

It's clear that the cloud computing market is poised for continued growth as more companies adopt it as part of their IT strategy. According to a research report from IT industry analysts at IDC, revenue from cloud computing is expected to reach over $44.2 billion by 2013.[14] Figure 6.3 breaks down the revenue from this segment according to product/service type.

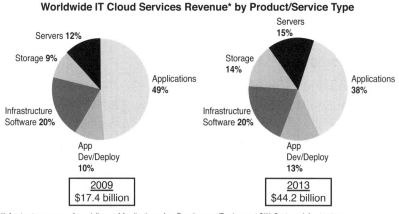

*Infrastructure revenue from delivery of Applications. App Development/Deployment SW. Systems Infrastructure
SW, and Server and Disk Storage capacity via Services model: AD&D excludes online B2B messaging providers/exchanges.

Figure 6.3   *Cloud computing revenue growth through 2013*

The immediate questions for many business professionals with regard to cloud computing are the safety and security of their data when it's not located on their premises. This genuine concern is why we are seeing and hearing more conversations about public versus private clouds. With private clouds, companies can reap the same benefits of the cloud model, but they don't share any of the applications with any other company, as is the case with public clouds.

Whether using a public or private cloud environment, the end user still needs to go through the Internet for information or applications that are located in one of those clouds. This further underscores the importance of a sound infrastructure to support the influx of network traffic.

As IT analyst and blogger Joe McKendrick pointed out, "Many organizations—and departments within organizations—are becoming both providers and consumers of services. Some organizations or vendors will still publish more than they consume, and others will consume more than they publish. But the lines are getting blurrier all the time."[15]

Should faulty software practices make their way into a cloud, they might impact a wider audience than a more traditional on-premises model of software ownership. Therefore, we need to be that much more diligent when it comes to developing the applications and services that will be accessed via a cloud.

The Mobile Cloud

Meanwhile, software developers are writing code specifically to support the growing demand for mobile applications, a market that is expected to reach $9.5 billion by 2014—an 88 percent leap from 2009.[16] To the average user, the mobile application runs just as it would on his or her laptop or desktop computer, yet all the power to run the application comes from the cloud, not the mobile device. Behind the scenes, this requires some tweaking to the code to make those applications accessible on the go.

Although 75 percent of today's mobile cloud-based application market caters to the enterprise user,[17] we can expect demand from the consumer market in the near future. This demand will be driven by technology innovations that are currently under way. They will make it easier to conduct commerce and banking transactions via mobile devices, resulting in the global accumulation of 6.5 billion mobile connections by 2014.[18]

The Full Spectrum

At the risk of oversimplifying the process, sending and transmitting data from device A to device B usually involves several different networks before the message reaches its final destination.

Whether one network is stronger than another is less important than the fact that speed and delivery are based on the frailty of the weakest link in the chain. Some networks are more reliable than others, but all are ultimately limited by the amount of available spectrum. In layman's terms, this means that there is a greater likelihood that we will have more trouble connecting and downloading through our mobile devices in the near future before the situation improves.

This issue was made clear when FCC chairman Julius Genachowski addressed an audience at the Cellular Telecommunications Industry Association (CTIA) conference in October 2009. He stated, "I believe that the biggest threat to the future of mobile in America is the looming spectrum crisis."[19]

To put things in perspective, as of December 2009, approximately 834MHz of total spectrum was available. However, the FCC believes that most of this will primary be taken by year end 2010. Making things a bit more complicated is Genachowski's prediction that total wireless consumption could grow from 6 petabytes a month as of November 2009 to 400 petabytes per month by 2013. This is the data equivalent of the entire written works of mankind from the beginning of recorded history in all languages—times eight.

You may wonder why we can't just make more spectrum available. Think of spectrum as a very busy city bus during rush hour, when only so many seats are available. Building new buses takes time and involves technology, business, and government. So some folks will get seats, others will have to stand for part of the ride, and still others will have to wait for the next bus.

The situation is certainly not as cut-and-dried as it may sound. The FCC's 2011 budget of $352.5 million includes a proposal for a National Broadband Plan for better and more widespread coverage and improved public safety. It also contains recommendations for indefinitely extending the authority of the FCC to auction spectrum licenses.[20] Although many of us may take for granted our constant connectedness, a very real threat is looming due to limited spectrum. It is holding back our ability to offer better-quality health care, emergency medical care, and education in many remote areas.

Sustaining an Infrastructure to Support Current and Future Technologies

In my conversation with IBM Senior Vice President Steve Mills about the broadband issue, Mills said, "We as a society are getting a lot of information from physical mobile devices and collecting and analyzing that information to make everyday things smarter. We need to get creative and make the infrastructure we depend upon work better and last longer."[21]

Two points are key to sustaining our infrastructures to accommodate the continued growth of the mobile market:

- Additional network capacity
- Improved infrastructures to support the network

Additional Network Capacity

As many IT and business professionals are aware, network capacity can be added in many ways. Separate from the spectrum issue, adding network capacity is about making the most of your existing network. It's like trying to pack a suitcase for a long trip where you need to take everything that's on your list, so you have to carefully arrange how it will all fit together.

Short-term improvements that we're likely to see over the next few years include offloading traffic via WiFi and femtocell or upgrading to the high-speed packet access (HSPA) standard. Longer-term improvements include the long-term evolution (LTE) fourth-generation mobile broadband standard and an optimized spectrum. Let me explain those industry terms from a more pedestrian point of view.

In basic terms, WiFi is short for wireless fidelity. Users with WiFi-enabled computers and mobile devices can access the Internet through a wireless network, which is separate from a fixed network. It's like having an additional faucet in your house. This can help offload the network strain, because users are spread out across a network or are on an entirely different network.

However, the busier the location in terms of people who want to jump on the wireless network, the harder it can be to access the Internet. The service providers are aware of this issue, and efforts are under way to create more hotspot networks to accommodate even more wireless access. For example, in May 2010, AT&T tested a WiFi hotspot pilot program in New York City's Times Square. AT&T wanted to address smartphone and device traffic and to test the feasibility of creating more of these hotspots without draining its already overloaded network.[22]

A femtocell is a small base station that can sit in your home or small business. It improves broadband connections for customers while improving the service provider's coverage and capacity. It does this by relocating communications activities from the licensed cellular spectrum to a less expensive wireless option of voice over Internet protocol (VoIP). If you've ever had a conversation through your computer using Skype, the Internet voice and video communications service, you've experienced VoIP technology. Figure 6.4 shows a femtocell.[23]

Figure 6.4   *A femtocell*

The HSPA standard allows for higher data transfer speeds and more capacity. It also reflects the latest innovations in making the transmission of data through a network as quick and efficient as possible.

LTE is the highly anticipated standard for mobile voice based on its global roaming capabilities across different operators. It is not the same as HSPA. In terms of growing interest in supporting LTE, 15 public safety organizations of the National Public Safety Telecommunications Council (NPSTC) have already unanimously voted to endorse it. They hope to build a nationwide, interoperable broadband network that will further enhance communications in the event of an emergency.[24]

Improved Infrastructures to Support the Network

These efforts to advance the network infrastructure to support the overall growth in Internet adoption and widespread mobile device usage could be hindered if the infrastructure that is supposed to support the network is fractured.

As Mills told me, this will not be easy, especially when you consider this comment from him: "So much of IT investments are allocated to maintaining the networks. You want to add to what's there without diminishing what exactly you can use, and you want to make your infrastructure require less maintenance and less repair."

Many variables are involved in addressing bandwidth, capacity, and spectrum availability. Software can't solve every network congestion problem, nor can it better fortify the physical pipes and wires that transmit messages. However, software can make the most of our existing infrastructures if applied appropriately. Various software applications and tools categorized under operations support systems (OSSs) and business support systems (BSSs) are designed to help telecommunications providers do the following:

- Optimize network speed
- Reduce traffic
- Prioritize traffic according to size
- Monitor capacity and performance
- Prevent dropped messages and calls

However, with evolving infrastructures, new standards, various applications, and services already on the network, upgrading to support the latest standards such as LTE or HSPA is not as simple as adding new technology. One of the biggest challenges is that wireless networks typically contain various tools, components, and software from different vendors. Sometimes these technologies can be easily integrated, and other times they can't.

As new technologies are introduced to accommodate the growth in mobile connectivity, applying IT governance practices to software development can improve the integrity of the network infrastructure. This applies to the vendor developing the OSSs/BSSs as well as the company that is aiming to upgrade its network. In this regard, IT governance can support the development of the software that is critical to sustaining the wireless network. More specifically, it can help do the following:

- Maximize network capacity by identifying gaps or redundancies that lead to congestion

- Ease integration of new technologies by proactively identifying development errors before they become part of the final code

- Illustrate the impact of changes on the infrastructure before the new system goes live

Cruise Control in the Fast Lane

There's no stopping the amount of data that continues to be generated on a daily basis, and our reliance on mobile technology will only increase. For companies that want to better manage customer expectations from a business and consumer perspective, the following four actions are recommended:

- Initiate consumer and employee education efforts with regard to how we may be inadvertently straining the network when we unnecessarily run data-intensive applications on our mobile devices. This doesn't mean that we shouldn't continue to use these devices; it means that we need to be aware of when they're actively pulling from the network, unbeknownst to us. I liken this to leaving the lights on in your home all day when you won't be there.

- Conduct a thorough evaluation of the current state of the IT infrastructure and readiness to support new industry standards. This includes streamlining unnecessary traffic patterns that exist in the network, addressing redundancies in software and tools, and mapping the necessary integration efforts that will need to be executed.

- Actively participate in industry standards bodies to help steer direction where appropriate and to better prepare for the pending infrastructure changes.

- Elevate the role of IT governance to support the increase in exchanges that will take place in the cloud, through social networks and company collaboration tools.

As I think about the mobile industry, I recall the first time I saw a cell phone, which was probably back in the 1980s. It was about the size of a tennis shoe, weighed about as much as a college textbook, and cost about $1,000.

When I think about how far we've come in mobile technologies in such a short time, I have an even deeper respect for the collective efforts that have enabled us to be more productive in our work, more efficient in our emergency responses, and more in touch with our families and friends.

Enabling these efforts to continue to flourish is the responsibility of all facets of the IT industry, not just the service provider or the mobile device manufacturer. It will require continuous commitment from leaders across business, technology, and government.

Endnotes

1. Gartner. "Competitive Landscape: Mobile Devices, Worldwide, 4Q09 and 2009."

2. Morgan Stanley. "Mobile Internet Report." December 2009.

3. Blogband: The Official Blog of the National Broadband Plan. "Message from the iPad: Heavy Traffic Ahead." http://blog.broadband.gov/blog/index.jsp?entryId=138385.

4. Morgan Stanley. "Mobile Internet Report." December 2009.

5. J.D. Power and Associates 2010 Wireless Call Quality Performance Study, Volume 1.

6. *New York Times*. "AT&T to Urge Customers to Use Less Wireless Data." Jenna Wortham. December 9, 2009.

7. AT&T Fact Sheet. Network Performance. http://www.att.com/Common/merger/files/pdf/AT&TNetworkPerformance.pdf.

8. AT&T. UBS 37th Annual Global Media and Communications Conference. December 9, 2009.

9. The Secret Diary of Steve Jobs. http://www.fakesteve.net/2009/12/operation-chokehold.html.

10. ABC News. "Operation Chokehold": Did iPhone Protest Against AT&T Succeed?

11. Telework Trendlines™ 2009 Report. WorldatWork.org.

12. Minnesota Department of Transportation. National Transportation Safety Board Investigation. November 14, 2008. http://www.dot.state.mn.us/i35wbridge/.

13. Associated Press. "Cops: Computer glitch led to wrong address." March 19, 2010.

14. International Data Corporation. "IDC's Cloud Services: Global Overview." September 2009.

15. Interview with Joe McKendrick by Jeff Papows. February 2010.

16. Juniper Research. "Mobile Cloud Applications & Services: Monetising Enterprise and Consumer Markets 2009–2014." January 2, 2010.

17. Ibid.

18. Gartner press release. Gartner Highlights Key Predictions for IT Organizations and Users in 2010 and Beyond. January 13, 2010.

19. CTIA IT & Entertainment Conference. Keynote: Julius Genachowski. October 7, 2009.

20. Federal Communications Commission. National Broadband Plan. http://www.broadband.gov.

21. Interview with Steve Mills by Jeff Papows. December 2009.

22. AT&T press release. AT&T Launches Pilot Wi-Fi Project in Times Square. May 25, 2010.

23. Picture of Motorola femtocell. Source: Motorola.

24. National Public Safety Telecommunications Council press release. http://www.npstc.org/documents/Press_Release_NPSTC_Endorses_LTE_Standard_090610.pdf.

CHAPTER 7

Governing the Government

This chapter explores the role of IT governance in support of government infrastructures from the point of view of all three of these categories. Although hundreds of IT efforts are under way to improve governments around the world, we'll look at the influences of government on business, IT, and citizens from the broader perspectives of the following topics:

- The evolution of e-government
- The U.S. government's renewed focus on IT
- The government's role in the future of IT

When most people think about technology and the government, they usually fall into one of three categories—the casual yet savvy observer, the technology expert, or the business professional with a solid working knowledge of IT.

The casual observer sees the end result of technology in government, whether it's simply accessing forms through a website or engaging in sophisticated social media campaigns that helped elect local politicians, senators, and President Obama. In developing countries, the type of user might benefit from international programs and advances in technology aimed at closing the Digital Divide.

The Digital Divide is a major initiative by governments, businesses, and academic institutions throughout the world to close the gap between those with and those without the ability to acquire skills and gain access to digital information and the Internet through computers and broadband networks.

Regardless of the level of a person's interactions with government agencies, most casual observers would say that only when a glitch occurs do the complexities of the government infrastructure become apparent.

The second category of IT-in-government watcher is technology experts. They are more focused on the inner workings of IT in the government and making the massive behind-the-scenes complexities less complicated. This audience is more apt to focus on the interconnectedness and standards among agencies from a purely technical point of view.

The third group, business professionals, has a solid grasp of IT and the intricacies of governments and can apply business skills to improve those infrastructures. This type of experience will enable governments to maximize the world's collective investments in technology to better serve citizens.

The role of IT is slightly different in government because the principles of profit-generating businesses don't necessarily apply. Although vendors that provide technology products and services to government agencies can realize a profit, the goal of government is to provide effective services and deliver value to the public. Additionally, governments typically are held accountable to more regulations than a business because they deal with far more sensitive data and privacy requirements across various aspects of the populations they serve.

The Evolution of e-Government

In the 1990s, the concept of e-government really began to take hold. Technology and the rapid growth of the Internet fostered more open communication and the exchange of ideas among governments, citizens, and businesses. For developing countries, e-government also represented the promise of improved education and access to better health care and a wealth of services that may not have been accessible in more remote areas.

Since that time, great strides have been made through the use of technology in government in terms of streamlining what were traditionally paper-intensive administrative functions such as applying for licenses, contacting a local representative, or even filing taxes. Yet obstacles still exist to realizing the full benefits of e-government from the perspectives of greater transparency, collaboration, and efficiency. This is primarily due to a plateau in the return on investments and inconsistent approaches to IT architectures.

A Plateau in the Return on Investments

To some degree, an IT budget is relative to the size and scope of the organization it supports. According to Robert Holleyman, president and chief executive officer of the Washington, DC-based Business Software Alliance (BSA), the U.S. government is the world's single-largest customer of information technology and software.[1] Like any organization, the government expects a return on its technology investments in the form of productivity, cost savings, and more effective public offices.

Yet despite significant investments in e-government, the returns are starting to plateau. According to a 2009 report by McKinsey,[2] the three biggest obstacles holding back e-government are

- Ineffective governance
- Lack of web-related capabilities
- Reluctance to allow user participation in the creation of applications and content

Although it isn't in the McKinsey report, I'd cite a fourth obstacle:

- Global stimulus funds and continued investments

Ineffective Governance

Ineffective governance is usually the result of inconsistent approaches to enforcing governance practices, a lack of executive support, and a corporate culture that may undervalue the benefits that can be derived from governance. To reverse the effects of ineffective governance, McKinsey recommends that government agencies adopt a governance model where e-government efforts are owned by line-of-business executives and supported by a dedicated, cross-functional team.

This approach has proven successful in the private sector. Lynn Cox, a program manager at Ford Motor Company with more than 30 years of IT experience, sees it this way: "You have to demand that governance is followed through at an enterprise level where everybody follows the same processes. Otherwise, you won't have consistency across the board, and it leaves your infrastructure open to vulnerabilities. While you can't completely close that window, you can make it as narrow as possible through IT governance."[3]

Lack of Web-Related Capabilities

Without the ability to foster collaboration among citizens and include Web 2.0 capabilities on government websites, e-government initiatives will deliver diminishing returns. Advances from the private sector have conditioned us to expect higher-end web experiences. Therefore, when this same level of interactivity is unavailable on government sites, citizens will not return. This will add to the complexities that the old-fashioned paper-based methods of working with state, local, and national governments created.

Reluctance to Allow User Participation in the Creation of Applications and Content

Even when the government does catch up to the private sector's advancements in social media and Web 2.0 capabilities, its culture will need to adjust to those changes. This will be a challenge, because the mind-set among many agencies is to control the communications to the public. In the interests of privacy and national security, this is critical. But the ability for citizens to voice themselves through online forums and social media can't be overlooked.

Part of modernizing the government through technology is to embrace the innovations from the private sector without losing sight of the role that the federal, state, and local agencies play in protecting the public. Striking this balance underscores the importance of IT governance.

What government agencies should be mindful of as they embrace Web 2.0 technologies is the integrity of the applications and services that will be made available on their websites. Mash-ups are one area from the Web 2.0 world that is potentially ripe for glitches.

A mash-up is a combination of tools or data from multiple sources. Mash-ups typically collect data from multiple web pages and bring their information into one simplified web application.[4]

One example of a government mash-up is from the Bureau of Indian Affairs. This mash-up enables American Indians to complete an online survey about labor statistics within their tribes. This information is included in the Bureau of Labor Statistics (BLS) data and provides all citizens who access the BLS site with the most current information. In 2008, this data was collected by having American Indians fill out forms and fax them back to the BLS.[5]

Also, it would be impossible to overlook the efforts behind the http://www.data.gov website, which makes the government's massive sets of data available to the public. One of the primary goals of data.gov is to "expand the creative use of government data beyond the walls of government by encouraging innovative ideas."[6] Some of these mash-ups can range from charting childhood obesity rates by state, crimes by neighborhood, or the environmental health of a specific community.

The ability to quickly create applications that can serve different agencies is a boon to productivity. But without proper policies and best practices in place, those glitches may run rampant through the government. Furthermore, if the government data is used to create a mash-up for the private sector, who is accountable for a glitch? Odds are that the fingers would point back to the government agency, which doesn't have the infrastructure set up to test and certify third-party applications like the private sector does.

A recent discussion about mash-up capabilities in the private sector further brings this issue to light. Chuck LoCurto is the chief information officer and executive vice president of enterprise applications at Textron Financial, a diversified commercial finance company that is part of Textron Inc.'s $10.5 billion global network of aircraft, defense, industrial, and finance businesses.[7]

According to LoCurto, "Today, there is less line-by-line software development. By using mash-ups, open source software, and data integration tools, it can be quicker to assemble an application. What happens is that management sees the new application, gets excited about its capabilities, and may not realize that it hasn't been put through proper IT governance practices to ensure its integrity before it's released to the company." To this end, LoCurto believes that "IT governance is simply nonnegotiable."[8]

Global Stimulus Funds and Continued Investments

If there's one lesson we can take away from the financial calamities of 2008, it's that transparency is a requirement for transacting business in the global economy. Especially when you consider that by October 2009, 50 countries had committed $2.6 trillion to fiscal stimulus and pledged another $18 trillion in public funds to underwrite the financial sector and other industries.[9]

Before the financial meltdown, many efforts were already under way and investments had been made in fostering stronger e-government infrastructures and improving transparency. Some of these efforts include the International Telecommunication Union's (ITU) Connect the World by 2015 program. ITU is the leading United Nations agency for information and communication technology (ICT) issues, and Connect the World by 2015 aims to connect the world's unconnected.[10] Also, the United Nations' World Telecommunication and Information Society Day[11] and the Massachusetts Institute of Technology's IMARA project[12] are still actively trying to close the Digital Divide.

Aside from the stimulus package, Congress also allocated $35 million in 2010 to the U.S. Office of Management and Budget (OMB) for the e-Government Fund.[13]

While these efforts remain strong and are a vital aspect of making e-government successful, progress can sometimes be held back due to geopolitical issues and cultures that may not be as open to uncensored access to the Internet.

Inconsistent Approaches to IT Infrastructures

It's one thing to call for greater transparency and quite another to make it happen from an IT perspective. When you consider the complexities of a company's IT infrastructure, you know that hundreds of applications and web services can be strewn throughout the network. And you also know the challenge of trying to mesh two different infrastructures. Now apply that complexity times ten, and you realize how challenging it is to instill transparency across all government offices and agencies.

The challenges of creating successful e-government initiatives from an IT perspective are not unlike the challenges facing businesses in today's global economy. They include the following:

- *IT skills issues:* Developing countries do not have a stable of skilled IT professionals. Nor do they always have the required education curriculum available to train people how to build sophisticated websites, much less how to manage complex IT infrastructures. Additionally, areas with low literacy rates will be that much further behind in adopting technology.

- *Physical infrastructures:* In many countries, broadband access is still not at the speed or rate of efficiency that many of us take for granted in Western societies. The ITU reports that only 3.5 percent of the developing world has access to high-speed Internet.[14]

- *Silo approaches:* In lieu of being fully connected, governments are forced to build their own infrastructures. The integration efforts required to bring these agencies together will not be insignificant.

Here are some ways to address these issues:

- *Establish and enforce the use of best practices and policies* so that there is a consistent approach to establishing and maintaining infrastructures, which will save both time and resources.

- *Create reusable IT products and services* by using standards-based software. Additionally, the creation of templates and reusable web services will help contribute to the arsenal of technology tools and products available without requiring staff to create new applications from scratch.

- *Consider additional tax incentives to private industry* to reallocate physical assets and employee time to support e-government initiatives.

The U.S. Government's Renewed Focus on IT

One of the major platforms of the Obama Administration is using technology to create greater transparency across the government. Mandates are in place across nearly every agency to provide more visibility into the inner workings of the federal government.[15] One of the first directives put into place was the Open Government Directive. It is based on the principles of transparency, participation, and collaboration.[16] Essentially, it holds each federal agency accountable to specific action items to make their activities more visible to the public through the use of technology.

These three pillars of transparency, participation, and collaboration are applied to many IT efforts currently happening across the federal government—most notably, cloud computing. While we've addressed cloud computing in a general business and IT context, here we'll explore it from the perspective of the federal government.

Cloud Computing

On September 15, 2009, Federal CIO Vivek Kundra announced the government's cloud computing initiative and introduced the http://www.apps.gov website, an "online storefront for federal agencies to quickly browse and purchase cloud-based IT services, for productivity, collaboration, and efficiency."[17] Based on Kundra's remarks, it was clear that cloud computing would be the path to greater transparency and cost savings for the federal government. This cloud-centric path consists of the following:

- *Software as a service* makes software applications and web services available through a cloud as opposed to loading the full applications on every desktop or laptop.

- *Platform as a service* provides the environment to build and run applications, databases, and management systems.

- *Infrastructure as a service* makes computing resources available as needed to reduce energy consumption and related IT maintenance and management costs.

In terms of budgeting, an estimated $35 million of the Obama Administration's $79.4 billion IT budget for the year 2011 calls for the adoption of cloud computing.[18] The budget will help achieve the objectives set forth in the cloud computing strategy:

- Close the gap in effective technology use between the private and public sectors

- Reduce the number and cost of federal data centers
- Work with agencies to reduce the time and effort required to acquire IT
- Improve the alignment of technology acquisitions with agency needs
- Hold providers of IT goods and services accountable for their performance
- Improve the delivery of IT services

Federal agencies that do not adopt cloud computing will have to explain why. Agencies that fail to comply may risk losing their IT funding.[19] The reasoning is easy to understand when you realize that one study estimates that the government could save between 25 and 50 percent of its IT budget by moving to the cloud.[20]

Those cost savings will not be realized immediately, because the move toward a cloud infrastructure will take time. As Kundra wrote in his post, "We are just beginning this undertaking, and it will take time before we can realize the full potential of cloud computing."[21]

Achieving that full potential will require significant efforts across the government from an IT and cultural perspective. This is further evidenced by an April 2010 study conducted by Lockheed Martin. The study found that 70 percent of government technology decision makers in federal, defense/military, and intelligence agencies were most concerned about data security, privacy, and integrity in the cloud.[22] Along with those concerns are varying levels of awareness and adoption of cloud computing throughout the government. Figure 7.1 breaks down these various levels.[23]

More important in the context of outlining the hidden impact of faulty software, the role of governance has yet to be determined with regard to federal cloud computing adoption. Figure 7.2 shows the differing views among government IT and business professionals in response to the question "Who should govern cloud computing?"[24]

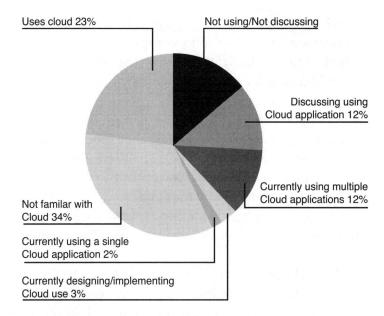

Figure 7.1   *Government state of cloud engagement*

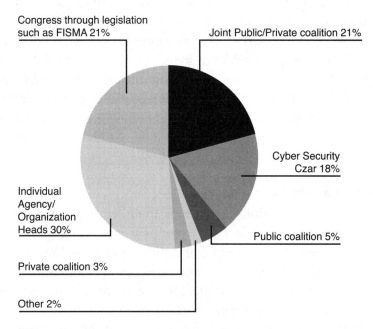

Figure 7.2   *Survey feedback to "Who should govern cloud computing?"*

To address some of these widespread concerns, the federal government's Interagency Cloud Computing Advisory Council created a joint authorization board that helps vet agency-wide cloud-based applications so that they can be more easily adopted by other agencies.[25]

By offering a form of governance through this overseeing board, federal agencies can accelerate their cloud computing efforts while reducing the risk of potentially creating and sharing faulty or unauthorized applications and services.

While the goals set forth by the cloud computing initiative may at first appear to be a daunting task, we likely won't see the entire federal government move to a cloud as a matter of privacy and security.

Kevin McDonald,[26] senior cyber security analyst for ICF International, Inc., a consultancy based in Washington, DC, explained that the cloud mandate means federal agencies will need to articulate how they'll approach cloud computing as opposed to putting every aspect of their infrastructure in a cloud. As the author of *Above the Clouds: Managing Risk in the World of Cloud Computing*[27] and as a member of the Tech America Cloud Computing Committee and the IAC-ACT Cloud Computing in Government committee, McDonald is entrenched in the government's cloud computing efforts. With regard to cloud adoption, McDonald believes that "it will be a while before it happens. And even then, you have to apply it where it makes sense."

Continued Open Source Momentum

It would be impossible to overlook the role of open source in government computing initiatives. Advances in open source have resulted in dedicated communities that foster the continued evolution of open source standards and protocols. For the government, this means greater access to technology at reduced cost without vendor lock-in.

Historically, the government has been a bit reluctant to embrace open source technologies due to the perceived fears of security breaches. But this mind-set is changing as the open source community continues to prove its value on an enterprise level.

Arguably, the nature of open source speaks to the Open Government Directive and reinforces the principles of transparency, participation, and collaboration. Yet fostering those principles and effectively applying open source technology to federal initiatives requires a level of IT governance throughout the entire infrastructure to ensure the quality of the code and its alignment with the agency's larger goals of serving the public.

The Government's Role in the Future of IT

The role of government in business is not exactly a new wrinkle. From the Roman Empire to the swashbuckling pirates threatening free trade on the high seas, history has countless examples of the government's stepping in to mediate and mitigate the potential risks to its country's economic stability. Today these issues are becoming more complicated when it comes to understanding the evolution of technology and its far-reaching implications for the future of society and business.

Three of the more complex issues are

- Overseeing the Internet
- Public safety
- The IT infrastructure as the path to the future

Overseeing the Internet

Here's a question that's guaranteed to start a debate: How much should the government be involved when it comes to the Internet as a vehicle of commerce? Although you likely formulated your opinion on that topic years ago, it's still very much a heated discussion both inside and outside the United States.

You may recall the Senate Commerce, Science and Transportation Committee working on the Cybersecurity Act of 2009. This bill essentially would have given the president the authority to shut down compromised federal or critical networks in the event of an emergency.[28] Although this hasn't come to pass, you can imagine the polarizing effects of the idea. As of June 2010, this issue was again raised as the "Protecting Cyberspace as a National Asset Act of 2010."[29]

Privacy advocates who closely monitored both sides of the issue raised the point that the government has not yet proven that it can do a better job than the private sector at securing networks. The obvious fine line is drawn when you think about government's role in public safety. I suspect we haven't seen the end of this bill, especially when you consider that attacks on a country are no longer limited to physical combat; more and more of them are occurring in cyberspace.

My intention is not to invoke riots by bringing up the topic of Internet regulation and the role of government in business. I raise the subject because on many levels we are affected by the government's role in technology. This includes a citizen's interactions with state and federal government agencies, large corporations that must adhere to government regulations set by the countries where they conduct business, and companies that directly provide products and services to the government.

Google Sets the Stage for Future Legislation

The significant role that government has played in business has become increasingly important since the Internet ushered in new economic models by helping level the playing field across the globe. Along with those models came unprecedented challenges and opportunities regarding overseas commerce. Still uncharted territory in many ways after all these years, we are likely to see the incidents of today evolve into major legislation in the near future as companies become more selective about how, when, and where they conduct business. Google is a good example.

In January 2010, Google found itself entangled in a very public issue regarding its operations in China. The previous December, hackers from China are believed to have broken into the Google corporate infrastructure with the primary goal of accessing the Gmail accounts of human rights activists, among others.[30]

The U.S. government got involved, and Secretary of State Hilary Clinton asked for a thorough investigation into the matter,[31] while the Chinese government denied its involvement in the attacks.[32] Exacerbating the situation was Google's public statement that it believed as many as 33 other major technology companies had also been hacked by the Chinese government.[33]

As the Google China story continued to make headlines, the search engine giant stopped censoring some search results, which was a stipulation set in place by the Chinese government in 2005.[34] This mutual violation of trust in agreed-upon business policies eventually led to Google's formal exit from mainland China in the spring of 2010. By July 2010, Google was back in China at least through 2011 according to the agreed-upon terms.

When we think of glitches, it's easy to draw a direct line between error and impact. However, the Google situation in China speaks to the need for greater visibility into the infrastructure to protect it from hackers and provide a sound platform for conducting business.

There are many different ways to view this situation from the perspectives of free trade, unrestricted Internet access, privacy, human rights, international treaties, and so on. On a global stage, this is the type of incident that can force new legislation regarding overseas technology ventures. While we don't want to create new laws as a knee-jerk reaction to negative experiences with overseas partners, we also want to protect ourselves as we continue to rely on a global infrastructure to sustain our businesses.

Public Safety

There is a real safety factor to be considered in the context of the intersection of technology in business and government.

Aside from the proposed Cybersecurity Act of 2009, there are networks and infrastructures that demand IT governance to protect and serve the public in the event of an emergency.

More specifically, emergency response technology is differentiated by its ability to bypass the existing network infrastructure when power lines and/or systems are down, thereby making sure the proper help is immediately available for citizens. In the event of an emergency, a sophisticated and glitch-free infrastructure enables local municipalities to dispatch emergency crews, alert hospitals, and bring in backup help if necessary. Yet this level of sophistication is not as widespread as one would hope. Despite the advances in technology, it is still very much a long-term goal for the majority of cities and towns throughout the world.

To make this vision a reality, local municipalities need to work with federal agencies. The good news is that a lot of work is already under way. According to Sue Levine, project manager of Regional Interoperable Communications at San Diego County Emergency Services, "I think the coordinated efforts are something that any region in any area can work on, but it really centers around governance and agency cooperation across many levels of government."[35]

As Levine pointed out, the Department of Homeland Security (DHS) has focused on working with state and local municipalities to ensure that people are working together toward a common goal. This common goal, from an IT perspective, requires a common platform. In fact, the 2010 guidance for the Urban Area Security Initiative (UASI) grants from the DHS requires adherence to the APCO Project 25 standard for public safety digital radio. The APCO Project 25 standard is aimed at standardizing communications among federal, state, city, and county agencies and vendors for public safety digital radio.

Additionally, public safety agencies have rallied around the long-term evolution (LTE) standard that we addressed in Chapter 6. To recap, this highly anticipated platform for mobile voice offers global roaming capabilities across different operators so that the network doesn't keep a message from reaching its destination due to incompatibilities in the infrastructure. LTE will be critical in the creation of a nationwide, interoperable broadband network.

The IT Infrastructure as the Path to the Future

Technology, in its purest form, will continue to connect people around the globe through computers and networks. As we've seen and will continue to see, technology is vital to supporting efforts around e-government, closing the Digital Divide, and protecting citizens.

From a much broader perspective, the IT infrastructure will also play a critical role in the economic development of nations. Here are some of these efforts that are supported by the government:

- *Agriculture:* Using technology to connect rural farmers so that they can share best practices with regard to climate, human environments, and day-to-day farming operations is critical to the sustainability of our food supply.

- *Water:* This involves enabling research to support purification processes and strengthen the infrastructures that literally make water available through a pipe. Today, dirty water kills more people than wars or other violence. Up to 60 percent of potable water is lost due to leaky pipes and poorly maintained sewage networks.[36] Much as we discussed in the section on providing better support for our energy supplies, technology can also play a role in fortifying and designing the infrastructures for the world's water supply.

- *Health care:* Providing technology resources to developing nations won't have a direct effect on curing diseases. However, making technology resources available so that health care workers around the world can communicate with and further educate each other is well worth the investment. For example, the Health InterNetwork (HINARI), led by the World Health Organization, gives public health workers, researchers, and policy makers access to the most current medical information from more than 6,000 journals and medical textbooks. A consortium consisting of representatives from businesses, academia, and government provides the information. Some of these members include the world's leading biomedical publishers, Microsoft, Yale University Library, and the U.S. National Library of Medicine.[37]

In these few examples, you can see how important it is to build a sound IT infrastructure to sustain and advance economic development throughout the world.

Next Steps

The strength of the federal government's infrastructure affects all of us in our business and personal lives. Although we need to protect intellectual property and data for security purposes, we also need to enable other countries to use technology to thrive. This might sound like a contradiction in terms, but it really isn't. True competitive advantage is not about tripping up the smaller players through faulty technology. Competitive advantage is about opening the channels of opportunity to businesses and countries that otherwise might not be able to compete.

From the view of the IT infrastructure, the following are recommendations to further complement the many efforts that are currently under way to support governments and citizens around the world:

■ *Create a global IT repository.* This repository of software tools, frameworks, and web services would be made available for free to developing countries so that infrastructures could be created more easily and quickly. The Global Governance IT Council that was suggested in Chapter 3 would oversee the repository. Their role would be to review, test, and certify the technology before it was made available in the repository so that users would be assured of its validity and quality.

- *Appoint IT governance leads at government agencies.* This senior-level position would oversee the IT governance efforts across an agency and would be responsible for assembling a cross-agency team to help ensure the creation and enforcement of policies and best practices.

- *Establish a global emergency network.* This is certainly an enormous undertaking. However, the concept of being able to more effectively connect different nations through a specialized network in the event of catastrophe is worth considering. There are, of course, many obstacles to making this a reality because of IT resources, capital, broadband availability, different flavors of mobile platforms, and so on. However, as each country looks at enhancing connectivity through standards such as LTE, it's not inconceivable to imagine a future with a separate global emergency network.

As we close this chapter on governing the government, I recall a conversation I had with Robert Holleyman from the BSA[38] about how we can all improve government infrastructures. He shared a terrific analogy regarding the institution of IT governance as part of the software development process.

Holleyman believes IT governance is very similar to how we learned to use the seat belts in our automobiles. As you may recall, this reflects the same thoughts shared by cyber security expert Dr. Jim Lewis. Both of these industry experts pointed out that before seat belts were mandatory, they weren't as widely used. As soon as the law required the use of seat belts, we had to remember to buckle up when we got in the car. Now the "click it or ticket" American catchphrase is stuck in our heads, and buckling up has become a reflex. Following the seat belt analogy further, we all realize that seat belts won't eliminate injuries, but they can certainly reduce the number and severity of injuries.

We should take the same approach to IT governance for the government in terms of building in security, policies, and best practices. The end result will be the most efficient, bulletproof software products possible that will better protect and serve citizens.

Endnotes

1. Interview with Robert Holleyman by Jeff Papows. December 2009.

2. McKinsey Quarterly. "e-Government 2.0." July 2009.

3. Interview with Lynn Cox by Kathleen Keating. February 2010.

4. WiseGeek. "What Is a Mash-Up?" http://www.wisegeek.com/what-is-a-mash-up.htm.

5. Washington Technology. "Mashups go mainstream as agencies mix data with social media." Rutrell Yasin. January 28, 2010.

6. http://www.data.gov. An official website of the United States Government.

7. Textron website. http://www.textron.com/about/company/index.jsp.

8. Interview with Chuck LoCurto by Kathleen Keating. May 2010.

9. United Nations E-Government Survey 2010. "Leveraging E-Government at a Time of Financial and Economic Crisis."

10. International Telecommunication Union. "Connect the World by 2015."

11. International Telecommunication Union. World Telecommunication and Information Society Day. http://www.itu.int/wtisd/.

12. Massachusetts Institute of Technology. IMARA Project. http://imara.csail.mit.edu/?q=about.

13. Office of Management and Budget. Office of E-Government and Information Technology. http://www.whitehouse.gov/omb/e-gov/.

14. International Telecommunication Union. "Measuring the Information Society 2010." February 2010.

15. The White House. Open Government Flagship Initiatives. http://www.whitehouse.gov/open/documents/flagship-initiatives.

16. Executive Office of the President. Office of Management and Budget. Memorandum for the Heads of Executive Departments and Agencies. December 2009.

17. Office of Social Innovation and Civic Participation. "Streaming at 1:00: In the Cloud." Posted by Vivek Kundra. September 15, 2009. http://www.whitehouse.gov/blog/Streaming-at-100-In-the-Cloud.

18. Budget of the U.S. Government, Fiscal Year 2011. http://www.whitehouse.gov/omb/budget/fy2011/assets/budget.pdf.

19. Channel Insider. "Feds Now Need to Explain Lack of Cloud Plans." http://blogs.channelinsider.com/cloud_computing/content/government/feds_now_need_to_explain_lack_of_cloud_plans.html.

20. Brookings Institution. "Saving Money Through Cloud Computing." Darrell M. West. April 7, 2010.

21. Office of Social Innovation and Civic Participation. "Streaming at 1:00: In the Cloud." Posted by Vivek Kundra. September 15, 2009. http://www. whitehouse.gov/blog/Streaming-at-100-In-the-Cloud.

22. "Awareness, Trust and Security to Shape Government Cloud Adoption." A white paper by Lockheed Martin, LM Cyber Security Alliance, Market Connections, Inc. April 2010.

23. Ibid.

24. Ibid.

25. Brookings Institution. "The Economic Gains of Cloud Computing." An Address by Federal Chief Information Officer Vivek Kundra. Washington, DC. April 7, 2010. http://www.brookings.edu/~/media/Files/events/2010/0407_cloud_computing/20100407_cloud_computing.pdf.

26. Interview with Kevin McDonald by Kathleen Keating. February 2010.

27. *Above the Clouds: Managing Risk in the World of Cloud Computing.* Kevin T. McDonald. IT Governance Publishing, 2010.

28. The Library of Congress. Cybersecurity Act of 2009. http://thomas.loc. gov/cgi-bin/bdquery/z?d111:s.00773:.

29. The Protecting Cyberspace as a National Asset Act of 2010. United States Homeland Security and Governmental Affairs Committee.

30. The Official Google blog. "A new approach to China." http://google-blog.blogspot.com/2010/01/new-approach-to-china.html.

31. Remarks on Internet Freedom. Hilary Rodham Clinton. January 21, 2010.

32. CNN. "China's Government Denies Involvement in Alleged Cyber Attacks." January 24, 2010.

33. The Official Google blog. "A new approach to China." http://google-blog.blogspot.com/2010/01/new-approach-to-china.html.

34. "Google May Quit China After Activist Attacks." Glenn Chapman (AFP). January 12, 2010. http://www.google.com/hostednews/afp/article/ALeqM5iNi073Lf9J3lIWZbddlt8FUsyX2g.

35. Interview with Sue Levine by Barbara McGovern. January 2010.

36. United Nations World Water Day, 2010.

37. World Health Organization. HINARI Access to Research Initiative. http://www.who.int/hinari/HINARI_INFOSHEET_ENGLISH_2009.pdf.

38. Interview with Robert Holleyman by Jeff Papows. December 2009.

CHAPTER 8

The Way Forward

Software will continue to take on an increasingly important role in supporting economic development, creating new revenue streams for the consumer market, and transforming how we work and live. To this end, the role of the software developer is one of the most critical functions in the organization. Without the technical skills of the software development community, business strategies cannot be properly executed, thereby affecting shareholder value. Yet across the organization, less than 10 percent of effectively formulated strategies are effectively executed.[1]

For these reasons, IT governance can be one of the most important bridges between successful business strategies and flawless execution of those strategies. Unfortunately, the term IT governance tends to stir negative images of an overseer looking for mistakes—whether it's a task force assigned to review software code or IT governance software that automatically identifies potential flaws. If we can shift those negative connotations to focus on the value that IT governance delivers in productivity and prosperity, we can begin to erase the negative connotations. This can be done through changes to corporate culture, approaches to software development, and an elevation of the role of IT governance to the executive suite.

This final chapter discusses the hidden impact of faulty software by focusing on the role of software developers. We will also branch out to the many areas of business that are affected by their actions. To do this, we'll cover the following topics:

- The rise of the software developer
- The responsibilities of managers and executives in mitigating glitches
- The way forward

The Rise of the Software Developer

In the near future, it is entirely possible that the role of the software developer will shift from a purely IT function to one where the scope of responsibilities will require solid business skills. This shift will be separate from the traditional role of the developer moving up the ranks into management. Instead, developers who demonstrate knowledge and who apply that knowledge from a business perspective will be rewarded beyond today's traditional compensation structure.

This will lead to the creation of a third branch in the developer career path. Most organizations today have two primary paths—the individual contributor and management roles. A third path would be purely technical, with a focus on software quality as it applies to the business. This role would not be responsible for traditional management activities such as budgeting and overseeing staff.

The expansion of the developer's role in the organization will also be driven by the following:

- The increasing demand for software developers
- Litigation and consumer action due to software glitches
- A transformation in the corporate culture

The Increasing Demand for Software Developers

As we discussed previously, opportunities for software engineers will increase by 21 percent from 2008 to 2018.[2] Compounding this need will be an increase in the volume of work required to support the continued instrumentation of products. This will result in a competitive and lucrative market for skilled IT professionals.

This demand will require that we be even more mindful of software quality as developers reap the benefits of the plethora of opportunities that will exist. We want to avoid a repeat of the dotcom era where jobs were filled by less-than-qualified applicants in the interest of making money for short-term gains. As we've learned from the stalwarts of the dotcom period, companies that focus on quality products and services can sustain themselves through bull and bear markets.

Litigation and Consumer Action Due to Software Glitches

Despite the upcoming strong demand for software developers, companies won't be duped by inferior efforts. They may even hold individuals or outsourcers accountable if they contribute to debilitating software glitches.

IT vendors will be held more accountable for faulty software due to:

- Changes in legislation
- Overseeing organizations and social media

Changes in Legislation

The Toyota recalls and the issues with overradiating cancer patients again raise the age-old debate about legal issues and responsibility for software development errors. This idea has been a somewhat polarizing topic in IT circles due to the nature of software development and the fear that liability may discourage those who are interested in pursuing a career in the field.

In 2009, the topic was brought into the courtroom yet again as the European Commission proposed that EU consumer protection laws be extended to "cover licensing agreements of products like software downloaded for virus protection, games or other licensed content."[3] When it comes to consumer products such as faulty microwaves or toasters, this law is enforceable. Yet in many cases, especially when it comes to enterprise software development, the biggest challenge is connecting a straight line between the software code and a glitch that results in lost revenue or worse. This is due to the many hands that touch the code—the customization that happens at the client site and various interpretations of the benefits the software will deliver.

Still, in May 2010 the UK High Court ruled that a software company was liable for buggy software. The case centered around the sale of hotel management software that didn't perform as expected. The hotel lost business and had to hire additional staff to fix the faulty software before it was eventually replaced.[4]

I don't expect litigation of this nature to become the norm. However, we can expect to see more cases given the sheer volume of technology that is now part of our lives. Be warned that lawsuits can be costly and time-consuming, and they don't always sufficiently address the main issue that usually leads to the lawsuit—the bad code.

Overseeing Organizations and Social Media

Since litigation may be an extreme measure, mechanisms are in place to oversee the quality of products. One of the more widely known certifications comes from the International Organization for Standardization (ISO), the world's largest developer and publisher of standards for business, government, and society.[5] Additionally, thousands of consumer advocacy offices, publications, and lobbying groups are committed to quality control and the rights of the customer. However, the majority of these organizations are set up to provide guidance and recommendations as opposed to enforcing standards.

For example, it's not uncommon to see ISO certification banners and plaques hanging in the lobbies of companies that manufacture goods. This certification acknowledges that the company follows ISO processes for product defect checking and applying appropriate corrective actions. The company also reviews procedures to determine and monitor their effectiveness and continuously improves its overall business processes.[6] However, obtaining third-party endorsement from the ISO is not a guarantee that the company's products won't be faulty. The certification only signifies that the company adheres to the recommended business processes set by ISO; it doesn't validate the execution of those processes.

Meanwhile, a wider quality gap is being created when it comes to the enforcement of higher standards for consumer products. This gap occurs largely because more consumer products are being infused with higher levels of technology and because no federal requirements are in place yet to account for the ubiquity of technology in all these devices. However, the efforts of the http://www.recalls.gov website shouldn't be given short shrift.

This government site is a one-stop shop for all government recalls. It is composed of six federal agencies that are dedicated to alerting people to unsafe, hazardous, or defective products: the U.S. Consumer Product Safety Commission, the National Highway Traffic Safety Administration, the U.S. Coast Guard Department of Homeland Security, the Federal Drug Administration, the U.S. Department of Agriculture, and the U.S. Environmental Protection Agency.

Although this website is a highly valuable source of information, the latest recalls.gov data doesn't always make it into the major news feeds. Otherwise, I'd argue that a good 30 percent more of our headlines would be about those recalls and warnings. We need consistent and effective approaches to spreading the word about faulty products beyond a website. One way to do this is by using social media.

For example, in May 2010, the Australian Competition & Consumer Commission (ACCC) released a report and accompanying recommendations regarding the process for reporting consumer recalls. It did so after discovering that consumer responses to product recalls varied widely and in some cases were nonexistent. In its recommendations, the ACCC suggested making greater use of social media, online communications such as websites and blogs, consumer alerts, and consumer reporting.[7] Vendors and consumers owe it to each other to fairly report product shortcomings in the interest of public health and safety.

Somewhere in the middle of litigation and accountability could be a sort of color-coded threat level system that warns customers that the software may be detrimental to health or safety. The coding system would be based on a set of criteria, and the labels would range from "formal complaints" to "pending litigation" to "resulted in serious threat or harm."

The ratings would be determined by customer feedback, posts on social media threads, and in-depth reviews of the products conducted by certified third-party reviewers. An overseeing body such as a Global IT Governance Council would ensure the validity and integrity of the ratings and make them publicly available on a website at no charge.

A Transformation in the Corporate Culture

With more emphasis on the role of software development practices to reduce the number and severity of glitches, the inevitable result will be a transformation in the corporate culture. Achieving higher-quality products and stronger bottom-line results will require a shift in how software developers view their contributions and how the organization prioritizes the development process. This will happen by:

- Getting developers on board with IT governance
- Understanding where the software goes awry
- Prioritizing IT governance throughout the company

Getting Developers on Board with IT Governance

In many instances, the developers' perspective of their contributions may be limited to the code or application they are currently working on—when, in reality, their contributions are far greater. According to Lynn Cox of Ford Motor Company, "You have to educate teams why IT governance is so important. You can do many things like mandatory training or tie it to performance reviews, but once someone really understands why it's important from a real-world point of view, that's when you start to see a difference."[8]

The bottom line is that IT governance simply will not happen if the developers and related IT teams are not on board. Following are recommended steps to make this happen:

- *Think like a developer.* Recognize that developers are primarily trained to build applications, troubleshoot infrastructure issues, and extend the value of software. Although they are focused on creating quality products, they don't always look at the bigger picture from a business perspective. Recognize that IT professionals strive to be part of something commercially competitive and important, and appeal to those interests as well as their desire to be engaged in the newest technologies. Understand these work styles and motivators, and accommodate them as you build the overarching IT governance structure.

- *Evaluate the quality assurance (QA) process.* Most QA processes are focused on testing the product to see if it performs accordingly. In the ideal environment, the customer perspective is taken into account, and the QA team puts the software through its paces just as a customer would. Time should be built into the product development and release schedule to include this critical step. From there, developers should be brought back into the loop so that they can see how the product performed under various user scenarios. This is different from simply pointing out bugs, because it puts the product into a real-world context to further educate developers and the QA team.

- *Test at every stage.* Make sure that testing is done at each stage in the development cycle so that errors are addressed immediately. Give the developers incentives by offering rewards for those who have the highest percentage of clean code. Offer testing teams rewards for the highest percentage of discovered bugs. If testing is done throughout the development process, the code will contain fewer bugs, and the software will have better quality overall.

- *Build governance into the production schedule.* As you map out the product's features and align it with a calendar, make sure that governance is instilled at the very first stage of the development process. This way, developers are on board from the onset of the project, as opposed to a last-minute rushed approach to reviewing the code.

- *Embrace mistakes.* Too often, the testing or governance review phases can feel like a cross-examination of the developer's skills. You want to discourage finger-pointing and foster an environment where an appropriate number of mistakes are tolerable as long as they are quickly identified and fixed and the same ones are not continuously repeated. You definitely want to avoid creating "counter bugs," which are essentially a defensive response to the review process. More specifically, a counter bug occurs when "someone reviewing your code presents you with a bug that's your fault, [and] you counter with a counter bug: a bug caused by the reviewer."[9]

- *Require clear, concise, specific bug reports.* This ensures that the issues with the code are addressed in a timely manner. Bug reports should not be complicated or convoluted, nor should they require additional resources to unravel their hidden meanings.

If you can streamline and automate some of the required processes associated with the software development cycle, the IT staff will be free to focus on the aspects of the job that are most appealing. They can create software that contributes to the industry's ecosystem and is viewed as a valued aspect of a business.

One more piece of advice for getting developers on board comes from Yakov Sverdlov, an IT professional with 30 years of experience in roles that span software developer, manager, and IT director: "IT governance should be a technical feature that is built into the software. This way, it is always running in the background, it is there when you need it, and it doesn't disrupt the software development process."[10]

Understanding Where the Software Goes Awry

We have addressed why it's important to improve software quality. But understanding how it goes awry is critical to shifting how it is designed, developed, and delivered.

If you've ever seen a screen full of code that at first looks like hieroglyphics, you understand how easily errors can get through the review process, especially when the reviewers are looking at hundreds of lines of code in a very short period of time.

Adding to this are antiquated software review processes. In many companies, more senior developers or managers review the code line by line after it's written and just before it's deemed "locked." This means that no more changes will be made to the code, and it is ready to be shipped.

Along with the monotony of much of the manual review process is the fact that in most organizations, more than one application or service needs to be reviewed, especially since new code will affect existing applications in the infrastructure. The sheer volume of code that needs to be checked lends itself to the frailties of human nature, which will inevitably lead to mistakes. However, many of these errors can be significantly reduced or avoided. Here are some of the more proven approaches:

- *Create centers of excellence (COEs).* COEs bring together practitioners with varied knowledge, experience, methodologies, resources, and best practices that can be applied to the software development process. Although proven approaches can save time during the review process, each application should be viewed separately, with an eye toward how it will be specifically used at the client site. Additionally, different views and experiences in software development should be encouraged as the COE is created or continues to evolve. Said Chuck LoCurto, CIO and executive vice president of enterprise applications at Textron Financial, "Two heads are better than one, but only if they think differently."[11]

■ *Automate appropriately.* Automating the more mundane software development tasks streamlines efforts while making the required last steps of the manual review process more effective. Often, a repetitive approach to manually developing software or reviewing code lends itself to more flaws. The developer or reviewer sees the same things repeatedly and may not find the subtle, hidden flaws that would be picked up in an automated system. This approach also frees the developers and reviewers to focus on the more complex and intellectually rewarding facets of the software development process.

■ *Apply software quality thresholds to business plans.* The quality of an organization is reflected in the products and services it puts into the marketplace. When companies have a clear idea of where to set the quality bar when it comes to the technology used to develop their offerings, they can formulate and execute more strategic plans that result in higher-value goods.

As IT industry analyst Dana Gardner of Interarbor Solutions suggests, "For companies to stop the proliferation of these glitches, they need to determine a business plan based on what they know the software—and the organization's levels of competency and governance—are capable of so that quality is already factored in. Software quality thresholds should increasingly be the starting point for business plans. And that means that the software quality thresholds should be known, governed, and managed, and hopefully always improving on an ongoing basis."[12]

Prioritizing IT Governance Throughout the Company

From a business point of view, the software development process should be more tightly integrated into the company's other line-of-business (LOB) functions. A CIO or vice president of engineering has a seat at the management table and reports on progress. However, more emphasis should be placed on the interconnectedness of the role of software development across the company as part of overall efforts to elevate quality.

Transforming corporate culture is not easy, but a 180-degree change is not required. Following are some recommendations for improving product quality through shifts in the corporate culture:

- *Include a segment on the role of IT during new-employee orientation.* Many of the learning modules in orientation programs focus on benefits or the new employee's specific job function. Providing a deeper view of the role of IT in the context of "why we're in business today" will give new employees across every department a greater understanding of the company's priorities.

- *Build incentives into development projects.* Hold developers accountable for the quality of their products by attaching bonuses to their efforts. The bonus structure should contain clearly defined metrics for uptime, reliability, quality, and percentage of errors.

- *Expose software developers to more LOB functions, and vice versa.* Try to foster better understanding among employees about how the individual roles contribute to the larger organization.

The Responsibilities of Managers and Executives in Mitigating Glitches

One message consistently came through during the majority of the interviews for this book. That message is that, although management understands and appreciates the value of IT governance, the majority of developers are less than enthusiastic about embracing it.

The key to making IT governance work effectively in an organization is to pinpoint the disconnect between management's perceived value of it and the reluctance with which it is actually executed on a day-to-day basis.

IBM Vice President Sandy Carter had the following suggestion: "IT governance has to be top down and across the board. The first step is for management to listen to developers and better understand their roles and perhaps some of their reluctance. Once that is understood, key stakeholders can collaborate on the best ways to introduce and enforce governance so that it is meaningful to the company and its customers. If you attach performance metrics and rewards to it, you'll see an uptick in the way governance is followed, but this will only be temporary. You have to make sure that the entire organization, from a technical, business, and cultural perspective, really understands what could happen if IT governance is not in place."[13]

If you're thinking that's easier said than done, you're not alone. The resistance to IT governance is warranted in some cases, but in other situations it has proven to save time and money. To address those concerns and provide a realistic view of what IT governance can and cannot do for the organization, the next sections look at the following topics:

- How to make the most of IT governance
- Supporting intersecting roles while avoiding duplication of effort
- Commitments and responsibilities
- Determining the criteria for success

How to Make the Most of IT Governance

There's no question that IT governance remains a top priority for CIOs. In the "2010 State of the CIO Survey" conducted by *CIO* magazine, IT governance was ranked third in the list of priorities.[14] Given its importance to the organization, the resources that are allocated to its successful execution should be closely monitored. However, this should be done without managers and developers feeling as if an additional weight is being added to their already heavy workload.

One of the keys to making governance effective is to "make it seamless and less intrusive and less knee-jerk." This advice comes from Professor M. Brian Blake, PhD, associate dean of engineering and research at the University of Notre Dame. He has more than 15 years of experience in consulting for government agencies and private organizations, as well as designing and teaching software development curricula.[15]

Key to achieving this seamless approach to IT governance is to understand the following:

- Audiences
- Requirements for transparency
- Ten ways IT governance is maximized, and ten ways it's squandered

Audiences

To make the most of investments in IT governance, it's important to recognize the key stakeholders:

- External auditors
- Outsourcers
- Service providers
- Partners
- Customers
- Business decision makers
- IT staff, managers, and executives

Given the many audiences that IT governance addresses, it's clear that it must move beyond the confines of IT. It also must meet business and technical requirements established by a company in order to be truly effective.

Requirements for Transparency

According to Christian Neau of Freeborders, an IT services organization headquartered in San Francisco, California, the requirements for transparency include an established set of metrics, assessments, and planning. Neau is responsible for IT governance efforts for Freeborders' externally sourced projects.[16] Here are Neau's requirements within those three categories:

Metrics

- Financial
- Quality
- Productivity
- Schedule and budget adherence
- Resources
- Service level agreement adherence

Assessments

- Customer perception with regard to satisfaction, value, and quick issue resolution
- Areas of targeted improvement

Planning

- Scoping of future sourcing activities
- Continuous-improvement plans
- Projections for projects, staffing, budgets

Without consideration for all the aspects of the business, IT governance efforts will fall flat. This is why it's critical to move IT governance from a back-room IT process to a company-wide effort. As IT industry analyst Joe McKendrick sees it, "IT governance is more essential than ever, since businesses rely on IT for everything, from managing production cycles to managing the employee lunchroom."[17]

Ten Ways IT Governance Is Maximized, and Ten Ways It's Squandered

According to IT industry veteran Yakov Sverdlov,[18] you can expect to spend approximately 20 percent of your IT budget on new development and 80 percent on maintenance. To make the most of these investments, following is a list of ten ways to maximize IT governance resources and a list of the top ten ways to squander those resources.

Ten Ways to Maximize IT Governance Resources

1. Hold frank discussions with developers about the value of governance, and address issues without fostering a fear of voicing opinions.
2. Create a cross-functional, company-wide IT Governance Council responsible for ensuring appropriate enforcement and aligning technology with customer priorities.
3. Establish benchmarks, and evaluate progress according to agreed-upon metrics.
4. Promote IT governance as a positive contributor to the company's bottom line, and offer employee bonuses to help negate unfavorable connotations.
5. Make each part of the IT infrastructure transparent.
6. Extend corporate governance policies to outsourcers.
7. Create reporting dashboards that reflect business goals.
8. Raise awareness of potential trends among employees or teams that may signal dissonance or gaps in skills.

9. Apply governance at each stage of the software development life cycle to avoid gaps that lead to glitches.

10. Automate where possible, but don't abandon the human review cycle.

Ten Ways to Squander IT Governance Resources

1. Enforce bureaucratic processes without explaining the context.
2. Include overlapping layers of oversight.
3. Create reports that nobody can understand.
4. Lock developers out of the code.
5. Take a department-wide approach.
6. Maintain a hyper focus on perfection.
7. Apply IT governance to only one aspect of the development cycle.
8. Don't track the cost and/or time savings IT governance provides.
9. Re-create similar policies.
10. Assume that existing IT governance resources cover compliance.

Additionally, according to M. Brian Blake, "You need to figure out ways to show the interconnections across different departments and across the organization. If you have dashboards to visualize the infrastructure, you get a clearer picture. That's a very difficult thing to do, but if you can figure out a way to do this, more people would get on board with governance."[19]

Supporting Intersecting Roles While Avoiding Duplication of Effort

If we can agree that successful IT governance requires cross-company effort, it stands to reason that each part of the organization better understands the others' roles and responsibilities. This helps reinforce the company's strategy with regard to IT governance and avoids duplication of effort.

The first step to achieving this is to create a Corporate IT Governance Council. As mentioned earlier, this overseeing council would be made up of representatives from each part of the organization so that the business and IT needs of the entire company are addressed. Depending on the size of the company, the Council could also include top customers and partners. As an adjunct to the Council, customers and partners would be invited to quarterly or semiannual meetings to provide feedback and help set future direction.

Echoing the value of the Corporate IT Governance Council, IT industry analyst Joe McKendrick says, "The best approach to introducing governance is through a cross-functional team representing major departments."[20]

To avoid duplication of effort, the Corporate IT Governance Council would also be responsible for the following activities based on its cross-company role that spans IT and business.

From an IT perspective, the following activities are included:

- Approving the creation of and any future software changes to IT policies.
- Determining best practices to be followed
- Evaluating and validating IT policies
- Managing and monitoring IT policies
- Providing realistic product development time frames and tracking them against associated costs per project

From a business perspective, the following activities are included:

- Coordinating governance efforts as they support compliance requirements
- Determining the soft ROI requirements, including productivity, performance, and customer satisfaction and retention

- Determining the hard ROI requirements, including costs of training, software, professional services, development staff, and related fixed costs

- Establishing realistic benchmarks to track hard and soft ROI

Commitments and Responsibilities

The level of commitment among senior executives and the Corporate IT Governance Council will be critical to sustaining its momentum and success. To illustrate the Council's importance to the organization, the following criteria should be in place:

- *Succession planning:* Sufficiently prepare for turnover on the Council, whether it's through attrition or retirement. Groom future members through training, periodic participation in meetings, and remuneration.

- *Anonymous employee feedback:* Although the Council is a fair representation of the entire organization, it is the Council's responsibility to solicit feedback from non-Council members to ensure a realistic view of the organization's activities.

- *Recognition by senior management:* Council responsibilities should account for no more than 15 percent of each employee's 40-hour workweek. It can't be considered an extracurricular activity or a volunteer position, or the results will be mixed. Senior management needs to recognize this commitment and hold the managers of Council members responsible for balancing their workload so that their primary jobs and Council responsibilities don't conflict. Additionally, the role of the employee on the Council should be factored into performance reviews.

Additionally, senior executives are legally responsible for providing transparency into the organization, whether it's for the purpose of financial reporting or adhering to compliance regulations. As you've learned, there is a fine line between legal responsibility, ethical responsibility, and commitment to product quality when it comes to taking ownership of headline-making glitches. Here are some ways to better address this:

■ *Require ongoing certification* for software developers and users of medical equipment if the technology is made to help address life-threatening illnesses.

■ *Invest in "unplanned" visits* by third-party evaluators who will extract random code for quality assurance purposes.

■ *Engage government agencies* such as the Federal Drug Administration (FDA) or Environmental Protection Agency (EPA), and lobby for the creation of additional certifications for IT vendors to validate their products and services.

It's also important to recognize that IT governance doesn't have a one-size-fits-all approach. The variables that will determine how much or how little governance is applied include corporate culture, industry, business model, size of the organization, percentage of offshore development work, and the like. Each company needs to weigh the factors most important to it and apply appropriate IT governance policies against them.

Ten Questions: A Checklist to Determine Criteria for Success

Kim Kazmaier, a senior IT architect with more than 30 years of industry experience, primarily in the financial services sector, believes that success with IT governance "begins with a commitment to execution quality from the top of an organization expressed in clear goals. These goals get refined into more and more measurable goals throughout the IT organization."[21]

These goals that Kazmaier talks about should be aligned with established criteria to determine the success of IT governance efforts. After all, in the near future, IT governance won't be an "if" question; it will be a "when."

Christian Neau, engagement manager at IT consulting organization Freeborders, collaborated with me on the following list of questions. They help determine the key criteria for success when it comes to evaluating the benefits of IT governance efforts and related investments:

1. Is IT governance supported and enforced by management?
2. Are developers on board?
3. Is IT governance viewed as a strategic corporate initiative?
4. Does it foster transparency and accountability?
5. Will it ease integration of new technologies or infrastructures resulting from a merger?
6. Does IT governance drive positive behavioral changes?
7. Does it provide value to all stakeholders?
8. Is it as lean and efficient as possible?
9. Would the infrastructure stand up to an unplanned audit?
10. Has IT governance resulted in the reduction of software errors?

The Way Forward

Until we reach the point where IT governance is fully automated and part of the fabric of the software development cycle, we will continue to read a steady stream of glitch-related headlines and see the financial impact on businesses, consumers, and society as a whole.

In the near future, we will see more widespread glitches. When their impact becomes impossible to ignore, business leaders will initiate more conversations about the quality of software development practices. This, in turn, will give rise to the need for more structured approaches to IT governance.

As we usher in this next wave of IT governance awareness, we need to avoid an extreme pendulum shift, much like we saw with compliance efforts such as Sarbanes-Oxley. Governance doesn't need to be a necessary evil or a bloated line item. The role of IT governance is to improve the software development process so that better-quality products are distributed to the market.

In the words of IT industry analyst Dana Gardner, "The power of modern software and services comes from a community and ecosystem of participants, variables, technologies, suppliers, and support. This diversity is both a strength and weakness. When a software problem leads to a donnybrook of finger-pointing, recriminations, dodges, denials, and failures to trace the causes and effects, then the breakdown is not technical. It is a governance breakdown. Rules of the road must be declared, distributed, understood, and enforced throughout the software life cycle, and this should not be different for software than it is for materials or supply chain-based manufacturing, or food processing."[22]

How we go forward from here will depend on a variety of factors:

- Executive awareness and support of company-wide IT governance
- Managers who enforce IT governance policies and best practices
- Developers asking for governance to help create better software products
- Customers demanding more stringent development processes
- Governments requiring well-defined IT governance thresholds
- Partners demanding validation of the quality of the infrastructure that they are intersecting

- Service providers guaranteeing the integrity of their cloud infrastructures

- Outsourcers adhering to quality controls established by the client

- Academia stressing the business relevance of IT governance in higher-education curricula

Let me sum things up with some final observations:

- We have a generation of best practices to draw on for the design, implementation, and maintenance of our competitive businesses. Let's turn our innovations inward and demand higher standards across the board in terms of software quality.

- We will constantly face increasing pressure to do even more with less. To get ahead of this trend, we need to equip our IT workforce with the training and technology that will enable all of us to avoid disruptions in the economy that are rooted at the keyboard.

- Streamline the infrastructure wherever and whenever possible to enable transparency at every level.

Innovation built the IT industry and made it a fundamental driver of the world's economy. Today, IT permeates every facet of our consumer and daily experiences. It is not just the critical substrate of our business; it's embedded in the fabric of our cultural existence. While there's no denying that technology has been a catalyst for positive change throughout the world, the reality is that in many ways, it's still in its nascent stages despite its radical impact on our personal and business lives.

I believe all the industry shifts described in this book represent an interesting challenge. It's a challenge that will push us technologically and intellectually, and we will continue to see positive outcomes from our investments in this industry as we collectively contribute to the next big thing.

I hope you found the facts and observations in this book eye-opening, thought-provoking, and meaningful. I also hope that, if you work in the IT industry, you will take pride in and outright gratification from the magnitude of your contributions to date and the lasting effects they will have on the next generation.

Endnotes

1. The Performance Factory. Strategy Execution Barometer. 2007 Executive Conference.

2. United States Bureau of Labor Statistics. Occupational Handbook 2010–2011.

3. Europa press release. Consumer Rights: Commission Wants Consumers to Surf the Web Without Borders. May 5, 2009.

4. OUT-LAW News. "Software company's liability clause was not 'reasonable,' says High Court." May 5, 2010. http://out-law.com/page-11011.

5. International Organization for Standardization.

6. International Organization for Standardization. Processes and Procedures. http://www.iso.org/iso/standards_development/processes_and_procedures.htm.

7. Australian Competition & Consumer Commission. "Effective recalls, better information, safer consumers." May 27, 2010.

8. Interview with Lynn Cox by Kathleen Keating. February 2010.

9. eWeek. "How to Speak Geek: Decoding Programmer Jargon." Darryl Taft. May 28, 2010.

10. Interview with Yakov Sverdlov by Kathleen Keating. April 2010.

11. Interview with Chuck LoCurto by Kathleen Keating. May 2010.

12. Interview with Dana Gardner by Kathleen Keating. February 2010.

13. Interview with Sandy Carter by Kathleen Keating. March 2010.

14. *CIO* magazine. "The State of the CIO Survey." December 15, 2009/January 1, 2010.

15. Interview with M. Brian Blake, PhD, by Kathleen Keating. January 2010.

16. Interview with Christian Neau by Kathleen Keating. May 2010.

17. Interview with Joe McKendrick by Kathleen Keating. February 2010.

18. Interview with Yakov Sverdlov by Kathleen Keating. April 2010.

19. Interview with M. Brian Blake, PhD, by Kathleen Keating. January 2010.

20. Interview with Joe McKendrick by Kathleen Keating. February 2010.

21. Interview with Kim Kazmaier by Kathleen Keating. February 2010.

22. Interview with Dana Gardner by Kathleen Keating. February 2010.

The following article is reprinted in its entirety
with permission from *The New York Times*.

January 24, 2010
The Radiation Boom
Radiation Offers New Cures, and Ways to Do Harm
By Walt Bogdanich

As Scott Jerome-Parks lay dying, he clung to this wish: that his
fatal radiation overdose—which left him deaf, struggling to
see, unable to swallow, burned, with his teeth falling out, with
ulcers in his mouth and throat, nauseated, in severe pain, and
finally unable to breathe—be studied and talked about publicly so that others might not have to live his nightmare.

Sensing death was near, Mr. Jerome-Parks summoned his
family for a final Christmas. His friends sent two buckets of
sand from the beach where they had played as children so he
could touch it, feel it and remember better days.

Mr. Jerome-Parks died several weeks later in 2007. He was
43.

A New York City hospital treating him for tongue cancer
had failed to detect a computer error that directed a linear
accelerator to blast his brain stem and neck with errant beams
of radiation. Not once, but on three consecutive days.

Soon after the accident, at St. Vincent's Hospital in Manhattan, state health officials cautioned hospitals to be extra careful
with linear accelerators, machines that generate beams of
high-energy radiation.

But on the day of the warning, at the State University of
New York Downstate Medical Center in Brooklyn, a 32-year-
old breast cancer patient named Alexandra Jn-Charles
absorbed the first of 27 days of radiation overdoses, each three
times the prescribed amount. A linear accelerator with a missing filter would burn a hole in her chest, leaving a gaping
wound so painful that this mother of two young children considered suicide.

Ms. Jn-Charles and Mr. Jerome-Parks died a month apart. Both experienced the wonders and the brutality of radiation. It helped diagnose and treat their disease. It also inflicted unspeakable pain.

Yet while Mr. Jerome-Parks had hoped that others might learn from his misfortune, the details of his case—and Ms. Jn-Charles's—have until now been shielded from public view by the government, doctors, and the hospital.

Americans today receive far more medical radiation than ever before. The average lifetime dose of diagnostic radiation has increased sevenfold since 1980, and more than half of all cancer patients receive radiation therapy. Without a doubt, radiation saves countless lives, and serious accidents are rare.

But patients often know little about the harm that can result when safety rules are violated and ever more powerful and technologically complex machines go awry. To better understand those risks, *The New York Times* examined thousands of pages of public and private records and interviewed physicians, medical physicists, researchers, and government regulators.

The Times found that while this new technology allows doctors to more accurately attack tumors and reduce certain mistakes, its complexity has created new avenues for error—through software flaws, faulty programming, poor safety procedures, or inadequate staffing and training. When those errors occur, they can be crippling.

"Linear accelerators and treatment planning are enormously more complex than 20 years ago," said Dr. Howard I. Amols, chief of clinical physics at Memorial Sloan-Kettering Cancer Center in New York. But hospitals, he said, are often too trusting of the new computer systems and software, relying on them as if they had been tested over time, when in fact they have not.

Regulators and researchers can only guess how often radiotherapy accidents occur. With no single agency overseeing medical radiation, there is no central clearinghouse of cases.

Accidents are chronically underreported, records show, and some states do not require that they be reported at all.

In June, *The Times* reported that a Philadelphia hospital gave the wrong radiation dose to more than 90 patients with prostate cancer—and then kept quiet about it. In 2005, a Florida hospital disclosed that 77 brain cancer patients had received 50 percent more radiation than prescribed because one of the most powerful—and supposedly precise—linear accelerators had been programmed incorrectly for nearly a year.

Dr. John J. Feldmeier, a radiation oncologist at the University of Toledo and a leading authority on the treatment of radiation injuries, estimates that 1 in 20 patients will suffer injuries.

Most are normal complications from radiation, not mistakes, Dr. Feldmeier said. But in some cases, the line between the two is uncertain and a source of continuing debate.

"My suspicion is that maybe half of the accidents we don't know about," said Dr. Fred A. Mettler Jr., who has investigated radiation accidents around the world and has written books on medical radiation.

Identifying radiation injuries can be difficult. Organ damage and radiation-induced cancer might not surface for years or decades, while underdosing is difficult to detect because there is no injury. For these reasons, radiation mishaps seldom result in lawsuits, a barometer of potential problems within an industry.

In 2009, the nation's largest wound care company treated 3,000 radiation injuries, most of them serious enough to require treatment in hyperbaric oxygen chambers, which use pure, pressurized oxygen to promote healing, said Jeff Nelson, president and chief executive of the company, Diversified Clinical Services.

While the worst accidents can be devastating, most radiation therapy "is very good," Dr. Mettler said. "And while there are accidents, you wouldn't want to scare people to death where they don't get needed radiation therapy."

Because New York State is a leader in monitoring radio-therapy and collecting data about errors, *The Times* decided to examine patterns of accidents there and spent months obtaining and analyzing records. Even though many accident details are confidential under state law, the records described 621 mistakes from 2001 to 2008. While most were minor, causing no immediate injury, they nonetheless illuminate underlying problems.

The Times found that on 133 occasions, devices used to shape or modulate radiation beams—contributing factors in the injuries to Mr. Jerome-Parks and Ms. Jn-Charles—were left out, wrongly positioned, or otherwise misused.

On 284 occasions, radiation missed all or part of its intended target or treated the wrong body part entirely. In one case, radioactive seeds intended for a man's cancerous prostate were instead implanted in the base of his penis. Another patient with stomach cancer was treated for prostate cancer. Fifty patients received radiation intended for someone else, including one brain cancer patient who received radiation intended for breast cancer.

New York health officials became so alarmed about mistakes and the underreporting of accidents that they issued a special alert in December 2004, asking hospitals to be more vigilant.

As this warning circulated, Mr. Jerome-Parks was dealing with what he thought was a nagging sinus infection. He would not know until two months later that cancer had been growing at the base of his tongue. It was a surprising diagnosis for a relatively young man who rarely drank and did not smoke.

In time, his doctors and family came to suspect that his cancer was linked to the neighborhood where he had once worked, on the southern tip of Manhattan, in the shadow of the World Trade Center.

Several years before, he had taken a job there as a computer and systems analyst at CIBC World Markets. His starting date: September 2001.

Diagnosis and Treatment

What Mr. Jerome-Parks most remembered about Sept. 11, his friends say, were bodies falling from the sky, smashing into the pavement around him. He was particularly haunted by the memory of a man dressed in a suit and tie, plummeting to his death.

In the days and weeks that followed, Mr. Jerome-Parks donated blood, helped a family search for a missing relative, and volunteered at the Red Cross, driving search-and-rescue workers back and forth from what became known as "the pile." Whether toxic dust from the collapsed towers caused his cancer may never be known, though his doctor would later say he believed there was a link.

Mr. Jerome-Parks approached his illness as any careful consumer would, evaluating the varied treatment options in a medical mecca like New York. Yet in the end, what led him to St. Vincent's, the primary treatment center for Sept. 11 victims, was a recommendation from an acquaintance at his church, which had become an increasingly important part of his life.

The Church of St. Francis Xavier in Manhattan, known for its social advocacy, reflected how much Mr. Jerome-Parks had changed from his days in Gulfport, Miss., where he was raised in a conservative family, eventually moving to Toronto and then New York, where he met his Canadian-born wife, Carmen, a dancer, singer, and aspiring actress.

In turning to St. Vincent's, Mr. Jerome-Parks selected a hospital that had been courting cancer patients as a way to solidify its shaky financial standing.

Its cancer unit, managed by Aptium Oncology, a unit of one of the world's leading pharmaceutical companies, AstraZeneca, was marketing a new linear accelerator as though it had Mr. Jerome-Parks specifically in mind. Its big selling point was so-called smart-beam technology.

"When the C.F.O. of a New York company was diagnosed with a cancerous tumor at the base of his tongue," promotional material for the new accelerator stated, "he also learned that conventional radiation therapy could potentially cure him, but might also cause serious side effects."

The solution, the advertisement said, was a linear accelerator with 120 computer-controlled metal leaves, called a multileaf collimator, which could more precisely shape and modulate the radiation beam. This treatment is called Intensity Modulated Radiation Therapy, or I.M.R.T. The unit St. Vincent's had was made by Varian Medical Systems, a leading supplier of radiation equipment.

"The technique is so precise, we can treat areas that would have been considered much too risky before I.M.R.T., too close to important critical structures," Dr. Anthony M. Berson, St. Vincent's chief radiation oncologist, said in a 2001 news release.

The technology addressed a vexing problem in radiation therapy—how to spare healthy cells while killing cancerous ones.

Radiation fights cancer by destroying the genetic material that controls how cells grow and divide. Even under the best of circumstances, though, it carries a risk, much like surgery or chemotherapy.

The most accurate X-ray beams must pass through healthy tissue to penetrate the tumor before exiting the body. Certain body parts and certain people are more sensitive to radiation. According to research by Dr. Eric J. Hall of the Center for Radiological Research at Columbia University, even accurate I.M.R.T. treatments, when compared with less technically advanced linear accelerators, may nearly double the risk of secondary cancer later in life due to radiation leakage.

When therapeutic errors enter the picture, the risk multiplies. An underdose allows the targeted cancer to grow, while an overdose can burn and cause organ damage.

While most radiation burns are mild, comparable to a sunburn, larger doses can damage the cells lining small blood vessels, depriving the skin and soft tissue of nourishment. The result is a wound that resists healing.

"Not only do you lose the blood vessels, but the tissue becomes chronically inflamed, which can lead to scarring," said Robert Warriner III, chief medical officer of Diversified Clinical Services, the wound care company.

After soft-tissue injury, bone death in the head and jaw is the second most common radiation injury that Diversified Clinical treats.

At their worst, radiation injuries can cause organ failure and death.

Dr. Salvatore M. Caruana, then a head and neck surgeon at St. Vincent's, gave Mr. Jerome-Parks another option: surgery.

"I wanted him to have laser resection," Dr. Caruana, now at New York-Presbyterian Columbia University Medical Center, said in an interview.

In the end, Mr. Jerome-Parks chose radiation, with chemotherapy.

His wife would later tell friends that she wondered whether St. Vincent's was the best place for him, given that the world-renowned Memorial Sloan-Kettering was nearby. But she did not protest. His mind was made up, and there was no time to lose. His cancer was advancing, and smart-beam technology promised to stop it.

A Plan Goes Wrong

On a brisk day in March 2005, Mr. Jerome-Parks prepared for his fifth radiation session at St. Vincent's. The first four had been delivered as prescribed. Now Dr. Berson wanted the plan reworked to give more protection to Mr. Jerome-Parks's teeth.

Radiation can damage saliva glands, and if saliva stops flowing, tooth decay and infections become a significant risk. Coupled with bone weakness from radiation, the simple act of extracting a tooth can lead to destruction of the lower jaw and ultimately its removal, doctors say.

Dr. Edward Golembe, who directs a hyperbaric oxygen chamber at Brookdale University Hospital in Brooklyn, said he had treated serious radiation injuries to the jaw and called them "a horrible, horrible thing to see."

Tasked with carrying out Dr. Berson's new plan was Nina Kalach, a medical physicist. In the world of radiotherapy, medical physicists play a vital role in patient safety—checking the calibration of machines, ensuring that the computer delivers the correct dose to the proper location, as well as assuming other safety tasks.

Creating the best treatment plan takes time. "A few years ago, we had computers that would take overnight to actually come up with a good treatment plan," said Dr. David Pearson, a medical physicist who works with Dr. Feldmeier's radiotherapy team at the University of Toledo. Faster computers have shortened that process.

"But we still need to be able to verify that what the computer has actually come up with is accurate," Dr. Pearson said. "The first time it tries to solve the problem, it may not come up with the best solution, so we tell it, O.K., these are the areas that need to be fixed."

A few months before Mr. Jerome-Parks's treatment, New York State health officials reminded hospitals that I.M.R.T. required a "significant time commitment" on the part of their staffs.

"Staffing levels should be evaluated carefully by each registrant," the state warned, "to ensure that coverage is sufficient to prevent the occurrence of treatment errors and misadministrations."

On the morning of March 14, Ms. Kalach revised Mr. Jerome-Parks's treatment plan using Varian software. Then, with the patient waiting in the wings, a problem arose, state records show.

Shortly after 11 a.m., as Ms. Kalach was trying to save her work, the computer began seizing up, displaying an error message. The hospital would later say that similar system crashes "are not uncommon with the Varian software, and these issues have been communicated to Varian on numerous occasions."

An error message asked Ms. Kalach if she wanted to save her changes before the program aborted. She answered yes. At 12:24 p.m., Dr. Berson approved the new plan.

Meanwhile, two therapists were prepping Mr. Jerome-Parks for his procedure, placing a molded mask over his face to immobilize his head.

Then the room was sealed, with only Mr. Jerome-Parks inside.

At 12:57 p.m.—six minutes after yet another computer crash—the first of several radioactive beams was turned on.

The next day, there was a second round of radiation.

A friend from church, Paul Bibbo, stopped by the hospital after the second treatment to see how things were going.

Mr. Bibbo did not like what he saw. Walking into a darkened hospital room, he recalled blurting out: "'My goodness, look at him.' His head and his whole neck were swollen."

Anne Leonard, another friend, saw it, too, on a later visit. "I was shocked because his head was just so blown up," Ms. Leonard said. "He was in the bed, and he was writhing from side to side and moaning."

At a loss for what to do, Ms. Leonard said, "I just stood at the foot of the bed in the dark and prayed."

In a panic, Ms. Jerome-Parks called Tamara Weir-Bryan, a longtime friend from Toronto with nursing experience. Something was not right, she said. Then, as Ms. Weir-Bryan tells it: "She called me again, in agony, 'Please believe me. His face is so blown up. It's dreadful. There is something wrong.'"

At Ms. Jerome-Parks's suggestion, Ms. Weir-Bryan said she called the hospital, identified herself as a nurse and insisted that someone check on Mr. Jerome-Parks. If anything was done, it was not enough.

The next day, the hospital sent a psychiatrist to speak to Ms. Jerome-Parks, according to the hospital. A couple of hours later, her husband received yet another round of radiation.

Overdosed on Radiation

The Times has pieced together this account of what happened to Mr. Jerome-Parks largely from interviews with doctors who had been consulted on the case, six friends who cared for and comforted him, contemporaneous e-mail messages and Internet postings, and previously sealed government records. His wife declined to be interviewed about the case, as did Ms. Kalach, the medical physicist, and representatives of Aptium, Varian, and St. Vincent's.

In a statement, the hospital called the case an "unfortunate event" that "occurred as a result of a unique and unanticipated combination of issues."

On the afternoon of March 16, several hours after Mr. Jerome-Parks received his third treatment under the modified plan, Ms. Kalach decided to see if he was being radiated correctly.

So at 6:29 p.m., she ran a test to verify that the treatment plan was carried out as prescribed. What she saw was horrifying: the multileaf collimator, which was supposed to focus the beam precisely on his tumor, was wide open.

A little more than a half-hour later, she tried again. Same result.

Finally, at 8:15 p.m., Ms. Kalach ran a third test. It was consistent with the first two. A frightful mistake had been made: the patient's entire neck, from the base of his skull to his larynx, had been exposed.

Early the next afternoon, as Mr. Jerome-Parks and his wife were waiting with friends for his fourth modified treatment, Dr. Berson unexpectedly appeared in the hospital room. There was something he had to tell them. For privacy, he took Mr. Jerome-Parks and his wife to a lounge on the 16th floor, where he explained that there would be no more radiation.

Mr. Jerome-Parks had been seriously overdosed, they were told, and because of the mistake, his prognosis was dire.

Stunned and distraught, Ms. Jerome-Parks left the hospital and went to their church, a few blocks away. "She didn't know where else to go," recalled Ms. Leonard, their friend.

The next day, Ms. Jerome-Parks asked two other friends, Nancy Lorence and Linda Giuliano, a social worker, to sit in on a meeting with Dr. Berson and other hospital officials.

During the meeting, the medical team took responsibility for what happened but could only speculate about the patient's fate. They knew the short-term effects of acute radiation toxicity: burned skin, nausea, dry mouth, difficulty swallowing, loss of taste, swelling of the tongue, ear pain and hair loss. Beyond that, it was anyone's guess when the more serious life-threatening symptoms would emerge.

"They were really holding their breath because it was the brain stem and he could end up a paraplegic and on a respirator," Ms. Giuliano said.

Ms. Lorence added: "I don't really think they expected Scott to live more than two months or three months."

The group was told that doctors were already searching for tips on how to manage what promised to be a harrowing journey not only for the patient and his family, but also for the physicians and staff members involved in his care.

The full investigation into why Mr. Jerome-Parks had received seven times his prescribed dose would come later. For now, there was nothing left to say.

As Dr. Berson rose to leave the room, Ms. Lorence noticed that his back was soaked in sweat.

A Warning Goes Unheeded

Rene Jn-Charles remembers where he was and how she looked on that joyful day—his wife, Alexandra, the mother of their two young children, in brown jeans and a brown top, standing in front of him at the corner of Lincoln Place and Utica Avenue in the Crown Heights neighborhood of Brooklyn.

"Babes," she said. "I have no cancer. I am free."

Her doctor had called with the good news, she said. A seemingly unbearable weight had been lifted. Now after breast surgery and chemotherapy, she faced only radiation, although 28 days of it.

Ms. Jn-Charles had been treated for an aggressive form of breast cancer at a hospital with a very different patient profile from the one selected by Mr. Jerome-Parks. Unlike St. Vincent's, on the edge of Greenwich Village, the Downstate Medical Center's University Hospital of Brooklyn is owned by the state and draws patients from some of Brooklyn's poorer neighborhoods.

Ms. Jn-Charles's treatment plan also called for a linear accelerator. But instead of a multileaf collimator, it used a simpler beam-modifying device called a wedge, a metallic block that acts as a filter.

In the four years before Ms. Jn-Charles began treatment, 21 accidents in New York State were linked to beam-modifying devices, including wedges, records show.

On April 19, 2005, the day Ms. Jn-Charles showed up for her first radiation treatment, state health officials were still so worried about what had happened to Mr. Jerome-Parks that they issued an alert, reminding operators of linear accelerators "of the absolute necessity to verify that the radiation field is of the appropriate size and shape prior to the patient's first treatment."

In legal papers before she died, Ms. Jn-Charles explained how the radiation therapist had told her not to worry. "It's not painful—that it's just like an X-ray," she said she was told. "There may be a little reaction to the skin. It may break out a little, and that was basically it."

"A Big Hole in My Chest"

For a while, all seemed well. Then, toward the end of therapy, Ms. Jn-Charles began to develop a sore on her chest. It seemed to get worse by the day. "I noticed skin breaking out," she would later say. "It was peeling. It started small but it quickly increased."

When Ms. Jn-Charles showed up for her 28th and final treatment, the therapist took her to see Dr. Alan Schulsinger, a radiation oncologist. "He just said that they wouldn't give me any radiation today, and he gave me the ointment and stuff and said go home and come back in a couple of days," Ms. Jn-Charles said.

A couple of days later, she returned. "More skin was peeling off, and going down into the flesh," Ms. Jn-Charles said. Once again, she was told to go home and return later.

On June 8, 2005, the hospital called her at home, requesting that she come in because the doctors needed to talk to her. Fourteen days after her last treatment, the hospital decided to look into the possible causes of her injury, hospital records show.

It did not take long. The linear accelerator was missing a vital command—to insert the wedge. Without it, the oncology team had been mistakenly scalding Ms. Jn-Charles with three and a half times the prescribed radiation dose during each session.

At the hospital, doctors gave her the bad news, and later sent a letter to her home. "I am writing to offer our deepest apologies once again for the devastating events that occurred," Dr. Richard W. Freeman, chief medical officer, said in the June 17 letter. "There is now a risk of injury to your chest wall, including your skin, muscle, bone and a small portion of lung tissue."

Ms. Jn-Charles had been harmed by a baffling series of missteps, records show.

One therapist mistakenly programmed the computer for "wedge out" rather than "wedge in," as the plan required. Another therapist failed to catch the error. And the physics staff repeatedly failed to notice it during their weekly checks of treatment records.

Even worse, therapists failed to notice that during treatment, their computer screen clearly showed that the wedge was missing. Only weeks earlier, state health officials had sent a notice, reminding hospitals that therapists "must closely monitor" their computer screens.

"The fact that therapists failed to notice 'wedge OUT' on 27 occasions is disturbing," Dr. Tobias Lickerman, director of the city's Radioactive Materials Division, wrote in a report on the incident. The hospital declined to discuss the case.

The overdose resulted in a wound that would not heal. Instead, it grew, despite dozens of sessions in a hyperbaric oxygen chamber. Doctors tried surgery. The wound would not close. So they operated a second, a third, and a fourth time. In one operation, Ms. Jn-Charles's chest wall was reconstructed using muscle from her back and skin from her leg.

"I just had a big hole in my chest," she would say. "You could just see my ribs in there."

She saw herself falling away. "I can't even dress myself, pretty much," she said. "I used to be able to take care of my kids and do stuff for them, and I can't do these things anymore."

Her husband remembers one night when the children heard their mother crying. They came running, frightened, pleading: "Tell me, Daddy, what happened to Mommy? Say she's O.K., she's O.K."

For more than a year, Ms. Jn-Charles was repeatedly hospitalized for pain and lived with the odor of her festering wound. Meanwhile, her cancer returned with a vengeance.

Several months after her wound had finally healed, she died.

No Fail-Safe Mechanism

The investigation into what happened to Mr. Jerome-Parks quickly turned to the Varian software that powered the linear accelerator.

The software required that three essential programming instructions be saved in sequence: first, the quantity or dose of radiation in the beam; then a digital image of the treatment area; and finally, instructions that guide the multileaf collimator.

When the computer kept crashing, Ms. Kalach, the medical physicist, did not realize that her instructions for the collimator had not been saved, state records show. She proceeded as though the problem had been fixed.

"We were just stunned that a company could make technology that could administer that amount of radiation—that extreme amount of radiation—without some fail-safe mechanism," said Ms. Weir-Bryan, Ms. Jerome-Parks's friend from Toronto. "It's always something we keep harkening back to: How could this happen? What accountability do these companies have to create something safe?"

Even so, there were still opportunities to catch the mistake.

It was customary—though not mandatory—that the physicist would run a test before the first treatment to make sure that the computer had been programmed correctly. Yet that was not done until after the third overdose.

State officials said they were told that the hospital waited so long to run the test because it was experiencing "a staffing shortage as training was being provided for the medical physicists," according to a confidential internal state memorandum on the accident.

There was still one final chance to intervene before the overdose. All the therapists had to do was watch the computer screen—it showed that the collimator was open. But they were not watching the screen, and in fact hospital rules included no specific instructions that they do so. Instead, their eyes were fastened on Mr. Jerome-Parks, out of concern that he might vomit into the mask that stabilized his head. Earlier, he had been given a drug known to produce nausea, to protect his salivary glands.

Government investigators ended up blaming both St. Vincent's, for failing to catch the error, and Varian, for its flawed software.

The hospital said it "acted swiftly and effectively to respond to the event, and worked closely with the equipment manufacturer and the regulatory agencies."

Timothy E. Guertin, Varian's president and chief executive, said in an interview that after the accident, the company warned users to be especially careful when using their equipment, and then distributed new software, with a fail-safe provision, "all over the world."

But the software fix did not arrive in time to help a woman who, several months later, was being radiated for cancer of the larynx. According to F.D.A. records, which did not identify the hospital or the patient, therapists tried to save a file on Varian equipment when "the system's computer screen froze."

The hospital went ahead and radiated the patient, only to discover later that the multileaf collimator had been wide open. The patient received nearly six times her prescribed dose. In this case, the overdose was caught after one treatment and the patient was not injured, according to Mr. Guertin, who declined to identify the hospital.

"The event at the hospital happened before the modification was released," he said.

Mr. Guertin said Varian did 35 million treatments a year, and in 2008 had to file only about 70 reports of potential problems with the Food and Drug Administration.

Accidents and Accountability

Patients who wish to vet New York radiotherapy centers before selecting one cannot do so, because the state will not disclose where or how often medical mistakes occur.

To encourage hospitals to report medical mistakes, the State Legislature—with the support of the hospital industry—agreed in the 1980s to shield the identity of institutions making those mistakes. The law is so strict that even federal officials who regulate certain forms of radiotherapy cannot, under normal circumstances, have access to those names.

Even with this special protection, the strongest in the country, many radiation accidents go unreported in New York City and around the state. After *The Times* began asking about radiation accidents, the city's Department of Health and Mental Hygiene reminded hospitals in July of their reporting obligation under the law. Studies of radiotherapy accidents, the city pointed out, "appear to be several orders of magnitude higher than what is being reported in New York City, indicating serious underreporting of these events."

The Times collected summaries of radiation accidents that were reported to government regulators, along with some that were not. Those records show that inadequate staffing and training, failing to follow a good quality-assurance plan and software glitches have contributed to mistakes that affected patients of varying ages and ailments.

For example, a 14-year-old girl received double her prescribed dose for 10 treatments because the facility made a faulty calculation and then did not follow its policy to verify the dose. A prostate cancer patient was radiated in the wrong spot on 32 of 38 treatments, while another prostate patient at the same institution received 19 misguided treatments—all because the hospital did not test a piece of equipment after repairs.

In March 2007, at Clifton Springs Hospital and Clinic in upstate New York, a 31-year-old vaginal cancer patient was overradiated by more than 80 percent by an inexperienced radiotherapy team, putting her at risk for a fistula formation between the rectum and vagina. Afterward, she received antibiotics and treatments in a hyperbaric oxygen chamber.

In 2008, at Stony Brook University Medical Center on Long Island, Barbara Valenza-Gorman, 63, received 10 times as much radiation as prescribed in one spot, and one-tenth of her prescribed dose in another. Ms. Valenza-Gorman was too sick to continue her chemotherapy and died of cancer several months later, a family member said. The therapist who made those mistakes was later reprimanded in another case for failing to document treatment properly.

The therapist not only continues to work at the hospital, but has also trained other workers, according to records and hospital employees. A spokeswoman for Stony Brook said privacy laws precluded her from discussing specifics about patient care or employees.

Other therapists have had problems, too.

Montefiore Medical Center in the Bronx fired a therapist, Annette Porter, accusing her of three mistakes, including irradiating the wrong patient, according to a government report on June 1, 2007. Ms. Porter retains her license.

"We know nothing about that person—zero," said John O'Connell, an associate radiologic technology specialist with the State Bureau of Environmental Radiation Protection, the agency that licenses technologists.

Montefiore declined to comment. Ms. Porter, through her lawyer, denied making the three mistakes.

Fines or license revocations are rarely used to enforce safety rules. Over the previous eight years, despite hundreds of mistakes, the state issued just three fines against radiotherapy centers, the largest of which was $8,000.

Stephen M. Gavitt, who directs the state's radiation division, said if mistakes did not involve violations of state law, fines were not proper. The state does require radiotherapy centers to identify the underlying causes of accidents and make appropriate changes to their quality-assurance programs. And state officials said New York had taken a leadership role in requiring that each facility undergo an external audit by a professional not connected to the institution.

Two years ago, the state warned medical physicists attending a national conference that an over-reliance on computer programs might be leading to mistakes, including patient mixups. "You have to be ever-vigilant," Mr. O'Connell said.

The state imposed no punishment for the overdoses of Mr. Jerome-Parks or Ms. Jn-Charles. The city levied fines of $1,000 against St. Vincent's and $1,500 against University Hospital of Brooklyn.

Irreparable Damage

Mr. Jerome-Parks needed powerful pain medicine soon after his overdose.

Yet pain was hardly the worst of it. Apart from barely being able to sleep or swallow, he had to endure incessant hiccupping, vomiting, a feeding tube, a 24-hour stream of drugs and supplements. And apart from all that, he had to confront the hard truth about serious radiation injuries: There is no magic bullet, no drug, no surgery that can fix the problem.

"The cells damaged in that area are not reparable," Ms. Jerome-Parks reported to friends in an e-mail message shortly after the accident. National radiation specialists who were consulted could offer no comfort. Hyperbaric oxygen treatments may have helped slightly, but it was hard to tell.

"He got so much radiation—I mean this was, in the order of magnitude, a big mistake," said Dr. Jerome B. Posner, a neurologist at Memorial Sloan-Kettering who consulted on the case at the request of the family. "There are no valid treatments."

Though he had been grievously harmed, Mr. Jerome-Parks bore no bitterness or anger.

"You don't really get to know somebody," said Ms. Leonard, the friend from church, "until you see them go through something like this, and he was just a pillar of strength for all of us."

Mr. Jerome-Parks appreciated the irony of his situation: that someone who earned a living solving computer problems would be struck down by one.

He grew closer to his oncologist, Dr. Berson, who had overseen the team that caused his injury. "He and Dr. Berson had very realistically talked about what was going to happen to him," said his father, James Parks.

Ms. Jerome-Parks, who was providing her husband round-the-clock care, refused to surrender. "Prayer is stronger than radiation," she wrote in the subject line of an e-mail message sent to friends. Prayer groups were formed, and Mass was celebrated in his hospital room on their wedding anniversary.

Yet there was no stopping his inevitable slide toward death.

"Gradually, you began to see things happening," said Ms. Weir-Bryan, the friend from Toronto, who helped care for him. "His eyes started to go, his hearing went, his balance."

Ms. Giuliano, another of the couple's friends, believed that Mr. Jerome-Parks knew prayer would not be enough.

"At some point, he had to turn the corner, and he knew he wasn't going to make it," Ms. Giuliano said. "His hope was, 'My death will not be for nothing.' He didn't say it that way, because that would take too much ego, and Scott didn't have that kind of ego, but I think it would be really important to him to know that he didn't die for nothing."

Eventually the couple was offered a financial settlement, though it was not a moment to celebrate because it came at a price: silence. With neither of them working and expenses mounting, they accepted the offer.

"I cried and cried and cried, like I'd lost Scott in another way," Ms. Jerome-Parks wrote in an e-mail message on April 26, 2006. "Gag order required."

Now, the story of what happened to Mr. Jerome-Parks would have to be told by his doctors and the hospital, neither of which were part of the settlement. The identities of those who settled were not revealed.

"He didn't want to throw the hospital under the bus," Ms. Leonard said, "but he wanted to move forward, to see if his treatment could help someone else."

Dr. Caruana, the physician who had recommended surgery over radiation, added: "He said to let people know about it."

Friends say the couple sought and received assurances that his story would be told.

Mr. Jerome-Parks's parents were in Gulfport in February 2007, waiting for their house to be rebuilt after it was destroyed by Hurricane Katrina, when they got the news that their son had died.

Afterward, they received a handwritten note from Dr. Berson, who said in part: "I never got to know any patient as well as I knew Scott, and I never bonded with any patient in the same way. Scott was a gentleman who handled his illness with utmost dignity, and with concern not only for himself but also for those around him."

He ended by saying: "I commit to you, and as I promised Scott, everything we learned about the error that caused Scott's injury will be shared across the country, so that nobody else is ever hurt in this way. On a personal level, I will never forget what Scott gave me."

Dr. Berson no longer treats patients, said Dr. Josh Torgovnick, a neurologist who helped care for Mr. Jerome-Parks after the accident. "It drove him to retire," he said, referring to the fatal overdose. The hospital disputes that, saying Dr. Berson still sees patients at the hospital.

Dr. Berson did not respond to several messages seeking an interview about the case. Citing privacy concerns, a spokesman for St. Vincent's, Michael Fagan, said neither the hospital nor Dr. Berson would grant an interview.

In July, Mr. Jerome-Parks's father stood across from the beach in Gulfport where his son's friends had scooped up the sand they sent for his final Christmas.

"He taught us how to die," Mr. Parks said. "He did it gracefully and thoughtfully and took care of everything. Most of us would lose it. He didn't. He just did everything that he had to do, and then he let himself die."

Mr. Parks said he had thought about starting a campaign to make medical mistakes public—but he never did. Nothing would ever come of it, he concluded.

Simon Akam, Andrew Lehren, Dan Lieberman, Kristina Rebelo, and Rebecca R. Ruiz contributed reporting.

Index

FREE Online Edition

Your purchase of **Glitch** includes access to a free online edition for 45 days through the Safari Books Online subscription service. Nearly every Prentice Hall book is available online through Safari Books Online, along with more than 5,000 other technical books and videos from publishers such as Addison-Wesley Professional, Cisco Press, Exam Cram, IBM Press, O'Reilly, Que, and Sams.

SAFARI BOOKS ONLINE allows you to search for a specific answer, cut and paste code, download chapters, and stay current with emerging technologies.

Activate your FREE Online Edition at
www.informit.com/safarifree

> **STEP 1:** Enter the coupon code: AKBJZAA.

> **STEP 2:** New Safari users, complete the brief registration form.
> Safari subscribers, just log in.

If you have difficulty registering on Safari or accessing the online edition, please e-mail customer-service@safaribooksonline.com